Image to Word

Image to Word

ART AND CREATIVE WRITING

KATHLEEN WALSH-PIPER

A ScarecrowEducation Book

THE SCARECROW PRESS, INC.
LANHAM, MARYLAND, AND LONDON
2002

KH

A ScarecrowEducation Book

PUBLISHED IN THE UNITED STATES OF AMERICA
BY SCARECROW PRESS, INC.
A MEMBER OF THE ROWMAN & LITTLEFIELD PUBLISHING GROUP
4720 Boston Way, Lanham, Maryland 20706
www.scarecroweducation.com

4 Pleydell Gardens, Folkestone
Kent CT20 2DN, England

British Library Cataloguing in Publication Information Available

Library of Congress Cataloging-in-Publication Data

Walsh-Piper, Kathleen, 1947–
    Image to word : art and creative writing / Kathleen Walsh-Piper.
      p. cm.
    "A ScarecrowEducation book."
    Includes bibliographical references and index.
    ISBN 0-8108-4307-2 (cloth : alk. paper) — ISBN 0-8108-4203-3
(pbk. : alk. paper)
    1. Creative writing (Secondary education) 2. Art—Study and teaching
(Secondary) I. Title.

LB1631 .W235 2002
808'.042'0712—dc21   2002004721

♾™ The paper used in this publication meets the minimum requirements of
American National Standard for Information Sciences—Permanence of
Paper for Printed Library Materials, ANSI/NISO Z39.48-1992.
Manufactured in the United States of America.

11/22/04

Contents

Illustrations

Foreword

The history of ekphrastic writing is long, rich, and diverse, and for good reason: Since the time of Horace, if not before, poets and writers have known that the magic formula *ut pictura poesis* captures the natural confluences and parallels in the two art forms. Looking at art calls upon us to observe, taking in the particulars before the whole scene and its encompassing feeling. The act of writing imaginatively, whether poetry or prose, likewise first demands close observation—training the eye and getting the details right—before leaps of imagination can be made.

This training of the eye, something writers as well as artists must do, can take place by observing everyday life or by visiting an art museum. The museum may be an even better atelier for budding writers, because there they must learn to see their way into not only the known but the foreign. They must learn to transport themselves into, and recognize their reflections in, many cultures from around the world and throughout world history.

Poets in particular have always had a great affinity for both artists and art museums. In the twentieth century, Marianne Moore, William Carlos Williams, and W. H. Auden are among the many to have written poems inspired by paintings, artists, and museums. Guillaume Apollinaire, Frank O'Hara, and John Ashbery supported themselves by working as art critics and museum curators. Still other poets, such as Blaise Cendrars, Vladimir Mayakovsky, and Robert Creeley, have engaged in close collaborations with painter friends on illustrated books and art installations. Artists, in their turn, have created paintings inspired by poems, just as many artistic movements—romanticism, futurism, surrealism, and dada—have included both poets and artists. The inspiration is mutual and has a long tradition: To put it simply, surrounded by art, writers are in great company.

Kathy Walsh-Piper's book *Image to Word* is a testament to this inspiration and is a great introduction to the many ways writers can learn to write imaginatively from art. It is the product of many years' experience leading writing workshops in museums. Given the natural connections between art and writing, it is not surprising that many writing teachers across the country are working in art museums. Many are just starting out. *Image to Word* will be a great gift to them and will offer a new range of ideas to the experienced.

~CHRISTOPHER EDGAR

Acknowledgments

This book was written with the help of a Robert H. Smith Fellowship from the National Gallery of Art and an invitation to be a Museum Guest Scholar at the J. Paul Getty Research Institute. I would like to thank my colleagues at the J. Paul Getty Museum, especially Diane Brigham, Elliott Kai-Kee, and Shelly Kale, as well as Linda Downs, Janna Eggebeen, Heidi Hinish, Barbara Moore, and Julie Springer of the National Gallery for their support and suggestions.

I especially appreciate the thoughtful assistance and suggestions by Andrea Guidry, Amy Nelson, Carol Resnick, Catherine Proctor, and Acacia Warwick. Thanks also to Tracy Bays, Carolyn Bess, Jay Gates, Scott Gensemer, Ken Kelsey, Charles Venable, and Shin Yi Pi of the Dallas Museum of Art. Professor Samantha Hastings and Marsha Merritt of the University of North Texas made possible the production of the color CD. Many other individuals were helpful, and it would probably be impossible to name them all. But to the many teachers and museum educators who attended writing workshops over the years, and to Mitch Allen, Nancy Berry, Chris Edgar, Ed Sundt, Rick Sussen, Ron Thorpe, Bonnie Speed, Amy Lewis, and others, I would like to extend a note of thanks.

Special appreciation to my husband, Rubin H. Piper, who first developed this teaching method with me at the St. Louis Art Museum.

CREDITS

p. xxiv: Demuth, Charles. *I Saw the Figure 5 in Gold*. Courtesy of The Metropolitan Museum of Art, New York.

p. 3: Kupka, Frantisek. *Organization of Graphic Motifs II*. Courtesy of National Gallery of Art, Washington D.C.

p. 4: Rothko, Mark. *Orange, Red, and Red*. Courtesy of Dallas Museum of Art, Dallas.

p. 5: Bosschaert the Elder, Ambrosius. *Flower Still Life*. Courtesy of The J. Paul Getty Museum, Los Angeles.

p. 6: Greenwood, John. *Sea Captains Carousing at Surinam*. Courtesy of The St. Louis Art Museum, St. Louis.

p. 7: Close, Chuck. *Fanny/Fingerpainting*. Courtesy of National Gallery of Art, Washington D.C.

p. 9: O'Keeffe, Georgia. *Ladder to the Moon*. Courtesy of Collection Emily Fisher Landau, New York.

p. 11: van Ruisdael, Jacob. *Two Watermills and an Open Sluice*. Courtesy of The J. Paul Getty Museum, Los Angeles.

p. 13: van Hulsdonck, Jacob. *Still Life with Lemons, Oranges, and Pomegranate*. Courtesy of The J. Paul Getty Museum, Los Angeles.

p. 15: Gauguin, Paul. *I Raro Te Oviri (Under the Pandanus)*. Courtesy of Dallas Museum of Art, Dallas.

p. 16: Pollock, Jackson. *Cathedral*. Courtesy of Dallas Museum of Art, Dallas.

p. 17: Kline, Franz. *Slate Cross*. Courtesy of Dallas Museum of Art, Dallas.

p. 20: *Palampore*. Courtesy of Dallas Museum of Art, Dallas.

p. 21: *Sacred textile (mawa') depicting tadpoles and water buffalo*. Courtesy of Dallas Museum of Art, Dallas.

p. 22: Cole, Willie. *Household Cosmology*. Courtesy of Dallas Museum of Art, Dallas.

p. 23: Thiebaud, Wayne. *Cakes*. Courtesy of National Gallery of Art, Washington D.C.

p. 25: Munch, Edvard. *Starry Night*. Courtesy of The J. Paul Getty Museum, Los Angeles.

p. 26: Corot, Jean-Baptiste-Camille. *Landscape with Lake and Boatman*. Courtesy of The J. Paul Getty Museum, Los Angeles.

p. 26: Friedrich, Caspar David. *A Walk at Dusk*. Courtesy of The J. Paul Getty Museum, Los Angeles.

p. 27: Kandinsky, Wassily. *Improvisation 30 (Cannons)*. Courtesy of The Art Institute of Chicago, Chicago.

p. 29: O'Keeffe, Georgia. *Red Canna*. Courtesy of Collection of The University of Arizona Museum of Art, Tucson.

p. 33: Købke, Christen Schjellerup. *Forum, Pompeii, with Vesuvius in the Distance*. Courtesy of The J. Paul Getty Museum, Los Angeles.

p. 34: Church, Frederic Edwin. *The Icebergs*. Courtesy of Dallas Museum of Art, Dallas.

p. 35: Church, Frederic Edwin. *Off Iceberg, Newfoundland*. Courtesy of Cooper-Hewitt, National Design Museum, Smithsonian Institution Art Resource, New York.

p. 36: Church, Frederic Edwin. *Floating Iceberg*. Courtesy of Cooper-Hewitt, National Design Museum, Smithsonian Institution Art Resource, New York.

p. 37: Church, Frederic Edwin. *Iceberg, Newfoundland*. Courtesy of Cooper-Hewitt, National Design Museum, Smithsonian Institution Art Resource, New York.

p. 38: Catlin, George. *Prairie Meadows Burning*. Courtesy of National Gallery of Art, Washington D.C.

p. 39: Catlin, George. *The White Cloud, Head Chief of the Iowas*. Courtesy of National Gallery of Art, Washington D.C.

p. 40: Audubon, John James. *Passenger Pigeon*. Courtesy of The New York Historical Society, New York.

p. 41: Audubon, John James. *Carolina Parrot*. Courtesy of North Carolina Museum of Art, Raleigh.

p. 44: Caillebotte, Gustave. *Rue de Paris, Temps de pluie*. Courtesy of The Art Institute of Chicago, Chicago.

p. 45: Caillebotte, Gustave. *L'Yerres, Effet de Pluie*. Courtesy of Indiana University Art Museum, Bloomington, Indiana.

p. 46: Monet, Claude. *The Seine at Giverny*. Courtesy of National Gallery of Art, Washington D.C.

p. 47: Copley, John Singleton. *Watson and the Shark*. Courtesy of National Gallery of Art, Washington D.C.

p. 52: David, Jacques-Louis. *The Emperor Napoleon in His Study at the Tuileries*. Courtesy of National Gallery of Art, Washington D.C.

p. 53: Ingres, Jean Auguste Dominique. *Amédée-David, The Marquis de Pastoret*. Courtesy of The Art Institute of Chicago, Chicago.

p. 54: Rodin, Auguste. Jean d'Aire from *The Burghers of Calais*. Courtesy of Dallas Museum of Art, Dallas.

p. 55: Albright, Ivan. *Into the World There Came a Soul Called Ida*. Courtesy of The Art Institute of Chicago, Chicago.

p. 56: Cassatt, Mary. *The Tea*. Courtesy of Museum of Fine Arts, Boston.

p. 58: Burne-Jones, Sir Edward Coley. *The Pilgrim at the Gate of Idleness*. Courtesy of Dallas Museum of Art, Dallas.

p. 61: Raphael. *Saint George and the Dragon*. Courtesy of National Gallery of Art, Washington D.C.

p. 62: Martorell, Bernardo. *Saint George Killing the Dragon*. Courtesy of The Art Institute of Chicago, Chicago.

p. 64: Remington, Frederic. *The Advance Guard, or the Military Sacrifice*. Courtesy of The Art Institute of Chicago, Chicago.

p. 65: Watteau, Antoine. *Ceres (Summer)*. Courtesy of National Gallery of Art, Washington D.C.

p. 67: Fisher, Clarence S. Diary: *Archaeologist's Note*. Courtesy of University of Pennsylvania Museum Archives.

p. 68: *Necklace with Sekhmet Amulet*, Egypt. Courtesy of University of Pennsylvania Museum of Archaeology and Anthropology, Philadelphia.

p. 68: *Headdress Ornament with Heads Flanked by Crested Crocodile*, Colombia. Courtesy of Dallas Museum of Art, Dallas.

p. 70: de Chirico, Giorgio. *The Philosopher's Conquest*. Courtesy of The Art Institute of Chicago, Chicago.

p. 71: Cornell, Joseph. *Soap Bubble Set (Ostend Hotel)*. Courtesy of The Wadsworth Atheneum Museum of Art, Hartford.

p. 72: *Elephant Mask and Hat*, Africa. Courtesy of Dallas Museum of Art, Dallas.

p. 74: *Long-Beaked Bird with Crouching Figure and Masks*, Canada. Courtesy of Dallas Museum of Art, Dallas.

p. 77: *Takenouchi no Sukune Meets the Dragon King of the Sea*. Courtesy of Dallas Museum of Art, Dallas.

p. 78: *The Eight Immortals of the Wine Cup*, Japan. Courtesy of Dallas Museum of Art, Dallas.

p. 79: Rousseau, Henri. *The Waterfall*. Courtesy of The Art Institute of Chicago, Chicago.

p. 80: Avercamp, Hendrick. *Winter Landscape*. Courtesy of The St. Louis Art Museum, St. Louis.

p. 81: *The Unicorn in Captivity*. Courtesy of The Metropolitan Museum of Art, New York.

p. 85: Reed, Susanna. *Sampler*. Courtesy of Dallas Museum of Art, Dallas.

p. 87: Murphy, Gerald. *Watch*. Courtesy of Dallas Museum of Art, Dallas.

p. 88: Roesen, Severin. *Fruit Still Life with Champagne Bottle*. Courtesy of Dallas Museum of Art, Dallas.

p. 89: Holzer, Jenny. *I Am a Man*. Courtesy of Dallas Museum of Art, Dallas.

p. 92: Scholar's Desk. Courtesy of The Trammell and Margaret Crow Collection of Asian Art, Dallas.

p. 93: Keikai Gyokurin and Minagawa Kien. *Bamboo and Calligraphy*. Courtesy of The Trammell and Margaret Crow Collection of Asian Art, Dallas.

p. 101: Smith, David. *Cubi XVII*. Courtesy of Dallas Museum of Art, Dallas.

p. 103: Hepworth, Barbara. *Contrapuntal Form (Mycenae)*. Courtesy of Dallas Museum of Art, Dallas.

p. 104: Arp, Jean. *Sculpture Classique*. Courtesy of Dallas Museum of Art, Dallas.

p. 105: *Mughal Facade*, North India. Courtesy of The Trammell and Margaret Crow Collection of Asian Art, Dallas.

p. 109: Dougherty, George. *Champagne Glass*. Courtesy of Dallas Museum of Art, Dallas.

p. 115: Colville, Alex. *Horse and Train*. Courtesy of the Art Gallery of Hamilton.

Introduction

WRITING TRADITIONS

Great art and creative writing have something in common—poetry. Both create a metaphor, an image that is inexpressible. The images in great art and writing are often based on the same themes—from religion, literature, or myth. Often one will inspire the other. From the *pictura poesis* of Horace to the present, there is a long tradition of writing based on works of art, which is known as *ekphrasis*. The most well-known example of a poem based on a work of art is John Keats's "Ode on a Grecian Urn."[1]

"ODE ON A GRECIAN URN"

I

Thou still unravish'd bride of quietness,
    Thou foster-child of silence and slow time,
Sylvan historian, who canst thus express
    A flowery tale more sweetly than our rhyme:

(continued)

"ODE ON A GRECIAN URN" (cont.)

What leaf-fring'd legend haunts about thy shape
    Of deities or mortals, or of both,
        In Temp or the dales of Arcady?
    What men or gods are these? What maidens loth?
What mad pursuit? What struggle to escape?
        What pipes and timbrels? What wild ecstasy?

II

Heard melodies are sweet, but those unheard
    Are sweeter; therefore, ye soft pipes, play on;
Not to the sensual ear, but, more endear'd,
    Pipe to the spirit ditties of no tone:
Fair youth, beneath the trees, thou canst not leave
    Thy song, nor ever can those trees be bare;
        Bold Lover, never, never canst thou kiss,
Though winning near the goal—yet, do not grieve;
    She cannot fade, though thou hast not thy bliss,
        For ever wilt thou love, and she be fair!

III

Ah, happy, happy boughs! That cannot shed
    Your leaves, nor ever bid the Spring adieu;
And, happy melodist, unwearied,
    For ever piping songs for ever new;
More happy love! More happy, happy love!
    For ever warm and still to be enjoy'd
        For ever panting, and for ever young;
All breathing human passion far above,
    That leaves a heart high-sorrowful and cloy'd,
        A burning forehead, and a parching tongue.

IV

Who are these coming to the sacrifice?
    To what green altar, O mysterious priest,
Lead'st thou that heifer lowing at the skies,
    And all her silken flanks with garlands drest?
What little town by river or sea shore,
    Or mountain-built with peaceful citadel,
        Is emptied of this folk, this pious morn?
And, little town, thy streets for evermore
    Will silent be; and not a soul to tell
        Why thou art desolate, can e'er return.

V

O Attic shape! Fair attitude! with brede
    Of marble men and maidens overwrought,
With forest branches and the trodden weed;
    Thou, silent form, dost tease us out of thought
As doth eternity: Cold Pastoral!
    When old age shall this generation waste,
        Thou shalt remain, in midst of other woe
Than ours, a friend to man, to whom thou say'st,
    "Beauty is truth, truth beauty,—that is all
        Ye know on earth, and all ye need to know."

In more recent times, Charles Demuth reversed this process. His painting, *I Saw the Figure 5 in Gold* (figure I.1), is based on a poem by his friend William Carlos Williams.[2]

"The Great Figure"
Among the rain
and lights

I saw the figure 5
in gold
on a red
fire truck
moving
tense
unheeded
to gong clangs, siren howls
and wheel rumbling
through the dark city.

I.1 Demuth, Charles, *I Saw the Figure Five in Gold*, 1928, oil on composition board, 36 × 29¾ in (91.4 × 75.6 cm), The Metropolitan Museum of Art, Alfred Stieglitz Collection, 1949. (49.59.1). Photograph © 1996 The Metropolitan Museum of Art. All rights reserved, The Metropolitan Museum of Art

Artists and writers are kindred spirits and will often work in both genres, using one medium to stimulate work in their primary mode.

In *Just Looking*, John Updike's collection of writings on works of art, their creators, museums, and exhibitions, he reveals why writing about works of art is so natural. Updike's narratives travel back and forth from the image, to memory, to information, to sense impression, to appreciation of technique, but most of all, to the mysterious presence of a work of art. His chapter on children's book illustrations states that one source of this natural connection is picture books, our earliest linkage of pictures with stories. "The illustrator of children's books surpasses all other artists in the impressionability of his audience; what touches will produce an indelible effect is beyond calculation, no doubt, the receiving surface of a child's psyche being so soft and mysteriously laden and momentous with its raw energy."[3]

Kentucky writer Bobbie Ann Mason says: "It took me a long time to discover my material. It wasn't a matter of developing writing skills; it was a matter of knowing how to see things."[4]

Ekphrastic writing as a form of interpretation is well established in art museums. Museums as diverse as the Art Institute of Chicago, the San Francisco Museum of Fine Arts, the Menil Collection, the Detroit Institute of Art, and Reynolda House all have writing and publishing programs based on works in their collections. The Art Institute of Chicago recently published a volume of writings on their nineteenth- and twentieth-century collection entitled *Transforming Vision*, with writers such as Willa Cather, Carl Sandburg, and Saul Bellow. As poet Edward Hirsch writes in his introduction to that volume:

> Ekphrastic modes inevitably address—and sometimes challenge—the great divide between spatial and temporal experience, eye and ear, visual and verbal mediums. They brave the mystery dividing the seen from the unseen, image from text. They teach us to look and look again more closely. They dramatize with great intensity the proper response to a work of visual art may well be an ode or an elegy, a meditative lyric, a lyrical meditation.[5]

What this collection reveals is the mixture of observation and personal interpretation that writing encourages and a wide range of responses, from essay to poem, and the use of a variety of writing tools. For example, Mina Loy, in her poem "Brancusi's Golden Bird," uses synesthesia: "This gong . . . shrills with brass."[6] John Edgar Wideman, in writing about William Sidney Mount's *Walking the Line*, muses "Is that what I hear?"[7] Measuring the writers' responses against one's own creates new insight, which is exactly how this process works with a class or group writing in the galleries. This collection also reminds us that art is not always pretty, much less beautiful, and that the sobering realities of life, as well as its wonders, are recorded.

WRITING WITH IMAGES

This book is designed to capitalize on the power of art to afford unique experience. Writing about works of art is second nature for me because I have spent a lot of time looking at and thinking about art. This book really developed out of a game we played in the education office at the St. Louis Art Museum twenty-five years ago. I asked my colleagues to write a formula poem on one of the works in the museum collection that we knew well, then to see if we could guess which work the poem described. The results were startling for all of us because they were so expressive. So I began to integrate writing in the gallery with teaching in the museum, starting with modern art.

Museums can be intimidating. A group of teachers asked to discuss modern art could be very hesitant; but they are not hesitant to play a naming game or to write a poem. Using writing techniques for inter-preting modern art was very effective; partly because they helped the group simply to look at a work of art longer and more carefully, and partly because it made them realize that they "saw something" in works that had seemed incomprehensible at first glance. Because people are aware that there is a lot to learn about works of art, they tend to deny or dismiss their own ability to see and respond to the work. Writing about the work helps to dismiss that fear and to encourage more looking and more think-ing; it is an excellent method for teaching about art.

Writing about a work of art can produce amazing results. After many years of working with groups in museum galleries, I am con-vinced that there is a special synergy between writing and looking that is very creative. It is more than simple observation, description, or response. There is an interplay between the images in the mind's eye and the words themselves.

In trying to explain this effect, *poetry* seems to be the common denominator. Seeking the right words to express what the work of art conveys is to seek the inexpressible rightness or uniqueness that sets it apart. We express this poetry through metaphors, using words as touchstones for our reflections. Both the image and the form through which it is expressed combine to make a work of art—whether visual or written. Artists and writers share a sensitivity to reflecting upon experience.

The images they create hold the experience for us; the work of art holds a moment so we can examine and appreciate it. It also contains the artist's act of looking and making and beckons for us to consider it.

Writing about works of art really serves a dual purpose. Not only does the work of art provide a point of inspiration for the writer, but it also causes the viewer to slow down, analyze, and respond to the work and to become aware of the looking process. In a sense, it allows the viewer to "pay attention" to paying attention!

What I mean by *creative writing* is writing that springs from the heart and surprises us—writing that reveals something we know but had not fully realized or expressed before, writing that is inventive in its use of language. Conversely, the basis of good writing is observation, imagery, and perception. Books on "how to write" encourage close examination, comparing, and recalling skills that are enhanced by looking at art. If we want to write poetically, looking at art creates a frame of mind that is congenial.

Writing about art works best when done spontaneously in museum galleries because real works of art have a presence, a power to act as a catalyst for ideas and emotions. Although one can write while viewing art reproductions, the experience of actually writing in front of the work is very different—the actual experience resides in the object.

The special environment of an art museum is one where objects are "set aside" for contemplation. By its very nature it teaches attention and reflection, with the concept of looking as a separate activity. In fact, because the museum visitor must look without touching, the very act of looking and "feeling" with the eyes is intensified.

The exercises in this book are just a starting point, and although based on specific works, they can be used with many different works of art. The possibilities are endless.

TEACHING WITH IMAGES

Writing about works of art breaks down barriers to looking by asking viewers to *pay attention* to what they see and how they react. For museum educators, this method is one of many inquiry techniques that helps visitors to approach works of art, spend time with them, and feel more comfortable in galleries.

Historical and contextual information about art is important, but the best interpreters also find inventive ways to make the experience meaningful. One of the first steps is just getting people to *look* carefully and take time to see more. Creative writing activities help the viewer to attend to and become more aware of what is seen, felt, and thought. This process is based on encouraging careful observation and thoughtful responses.

Writing about works of art is valuable not only because the rich store of images in an art museum liberally builds and stimulates the imagination, but also because it teaches about art. Receptive and thoughtful attention, the most important skill for a writer, is also crucial for learning about art.

Although creativity and imagination are difficult to define and teach, research on learning tells us that we remember what is meaningful—what touches a chord or connects with our previous experiences. The more an idea is connected with our experiences and emotions, the stronger it is. The brain uses identical pathways for seeing objects and imaging them.[8] Memories are not stored whole, but are tagged by color, shape, and emotion in such a way that we can recall and recombine ideas and impressions to create something new. Literally, the store of images strengthens our capacity to imagine. The way to learn more about writing is by writing; the way to learn more about art is by looking!

Evaluation of creative writing classes in museums has shown that participants look more closely, understand the need to look closely in a new way, and learn from the comments of peers. The process enhances both the writing experience and the kind of attention given to the work of art.

Museum galleries present an opportunity for refocusing writers. Most of these activities work well with a group. By sharing results, writers see more, learn new interpretations, and begin to think about writing as a process.

There are several kinds of activities presented in this book. Although all should stimulate ideas for writing, they do not all equally teach about visual art. The best interdisciplinary approach is to focus first on writing, then use the results as motivation to teach more about the works of art. The works included here are examples; many different works of art can be substituted. If possible, write on the spot in your local museum or art gallery.

One criticism of interdisciplinary teaching is that art is used as an *illustration* for another subject, like social studies or language arts. But the activities here and types of art chosen are designed to both build observation skills and understanding of the visual language. It shares elements of two curriculum areas. This is the kind of learning where the interaction helps the student to make the knowledge his or her own. The process works as inquiry and makes subsequent learning about the work of art more accessible. Try asking a group of students to make a list of what literature does and what art does. Look for correlations!

The objectives of connecting art and writing in a shared curriculum are to teach:

- how artists and writers observe;
- the importance of attention to experience and observation;
- that both language and visual art are expressive;
- how to bring attention to form and expression;
- how to infer meanings;
- how to express an interpretation;
- that both artists and writers *show, don't tell*;
- that both artists and writers are involved in a long process to create a work, from the initial concept to sketches, drafts, critique, refinement, and the final work.

NOTES

1. John Keats, "Ode on a Grecian Urn," in *British & American Poets: Chaucer to the Present*, ed. W. Jackson Bate and David Perkins (San Diego, Calif.: Harcourt Brace Jovanovich, 1986), 480–82.

2. See H. H. Arneson, *History of Modern Art*, 2d ed. (New York: Prentice-Hall, 1975), 28.

3. John Updike, *Just Looking: Essays on Art* (New York: Alfred A. Knopf, 1989), 3.

4. "Bobbie Ann Mason: Zizagging Her Way Back to UK," in *Odyssey* (Lexington: University of Kentucky, 2002), 37.

5. Edward Hirsch, ed., *Transforming Vision: Writers on Art* (Chicago: Little, Brown and Company, 1994), 11.

6. Hirsch, *Transforming Vision*, 110.

7. Hirsch, *Transforming Vision*, 67.

8. Sandra Blakeslee points out that "neuroscientists have now found that the brain uses virtually identical pathways for seeing objects and for imagining them." Blakeslee, "Seeing and Imagining: Clues to the Workings of the Mind's Eye," *New York Times,* 3, August 1993, Science Times section, C7.

Breaking Down
Barriers to Looking

For many students, looking at modern art, especially if it is abstract, is daunting. In fact, there is a tendency not to look at all, but merely to dismiss this art. This series of exercises helps to slow down the looking process, makes the viewer aware of his or her own personal response to the work, and makes art less intimidating. It allows the writer to begin to find images in works of art. The goals of the exercises are first to describe and then to think metaphorically. For example, students can create a verbal metaphor for a work of art by giving it a name.

WARM-UP: METAPHOR

Take the group into a gallery where there are a number of abstract paintings or sculptures large enough for all to see, or use several large reproductions to "create" a gallery in the classroom. Ask the group to sit so they can see all the works in the gallery. First, forget art history! Do not give any introductory information about the works of art; don't mention style, artists' names, or anything that might set up a barrier to looking. Let the objects speak for themselves.

Say to the students: "We are going to play a game. I will be using these artworks [indicate specific ones—about six] as our subjects in the game. I will point to one of the works and also to one of you. Please give the work a name. It can be the first word that comes to mind." Responses to "naming" Kupka's painting *Organization of Graphic Motifs II* (figure 1.1) might be words such as: chrysalis, kaleidoscope, vortex, creation, butterfly. Your group might be hesitant at first, so keep things moving and respond positively to any answer at this point. If an answer is particularly creative or inventive, be especially encouraging. "That's interesting!" Keep going around the circle until the group starts to loosen up and you can see that the names they are coming up with are related to the images in the work.

Ask the group to try to recall and list all the names that were given for one particular artwork. Repeat for each work. Ask them to describe anything new that they saw in the work as a result of this experience.

Start the discussion by saying: "So, we each can see something different in a work of art, and we see more when we share our impressions." If there are similarities in the list for any work (such as, for Rothko's *Orange, Red, and Red* [figure 1.2]—sunset, fireball, explosion, hot tar, fudge—all of which are warm), discuss why. What is it about the image that prompted those words? Color? Line? Shape? Explore the ideas.

WRITING A POEM: METAPHOR AND SIMILE

Ask participants to mentally choose one of the six works of art, but to keep their choice a secret, as they will be writing a poem about it according to a structure. The group will be more comfortable if you tell them exactly what will happen—that the poem will have four lines and that you will give a prompt for each line. These are the prompts:

- First line: Ask students to give the painting a name, just as you did before—this makes for an easy transition.
- Second line: Ask them to write an action phrase, based on what they see, such as "running down the lane" or "flying to the treetops."
- Third line: Have them create a simile, a phrase using "like," for the painting.
- Fourth line: Have them give it another short name.

1.1 Kupka, Frantisek, *Organization of Graphic Motifs II*, 1912–1913, oil on canvas, 2 × 1.940 (78¾ × 76⅜), Ailsa Mellon Bruce Fund and gift of Jan and Meada Mladek. Photograph © 2001 Board of Trustees, National Gallery of Art, Washington D.C.

Ask each person to read his or her poem aloud while the rest of the group guesses the work that inspired it.

Here's an example based on Rothko's *Orange, Red, and Red*:

Glow
Closing the day at last
Like a warm stove
Restful home

1.2 Rothko, Mark, *Orange, Red, and Red*, 1962, oil on canvas, 93⅛ × 80⅛ in (236.54 × 203.52 cm), Dallas Museum of Art, gift of Mr. and Mrs. Algur H. Meadows and the Meadows Foundation, Inc. 1968.9, © 2001 Kate Rothko Prizel & Christopher Rothko / Artists Rights Society (ARS), New York

This activity works well with abstract paintings, but can also work with realistic works. Here is a poem created during a workshop for museum teachers at the J. Paul Getty Museum based on *Flower Still Life* by Ambrosius Bosschaert the Elder (figure 1.3):

1.3 Bosschaert the Elder, Ambrosius, *Flower Still Life*, 1614, 11¼ × 15 in (28.6 × 38.1 cm), The J. Paul Getty Museum, Los Angeles

Luscious loves
Seduce the eye and numb the nose
Like a delicious birthday cake
The secret affair between the dragon and the butterfly

                                    ~ADRIENNE WHITAKER

DESCRIPTION AND INTERPRETATION

Begin with a basic description. First ask students to look carefully and write what they see. One of the first things to learn about works of art is that there is more to see and know than meets the eye! But let's begin with what we see. Choose a work of art that you like or find interesting at first sight. Look at it for a minute. Now turn around and write about what you saw. Reread what you wrote and circle the most important things to you. How much of your description answers the key questions: who, what, where, why, and how?

Take a second look at the work. Do you see anything you didn't mention? Ask a friend to write about the same work and share results. Do you both see exactly the same things? What does the work bring to mind? Make a list of "I wonder" statements about the work. Now review your first description. Pretend you are writing this description for someone who can't see the work. How can you improve the description? Your goal is to create a "word picture" that will communicate the image you see, "painting" it with words.

Your description should be very factual by now. Now see if you can give a more interpretive slant to it by writing a poem in free verse, emphasizing the five senses: sight, hearing, taste, sound, smell, and touch. This activity usually informs the teacher about the group—how they see things, and how they approach an image. For example, a group of students completed this exercise with the painting *Sea Captains Carousing at Surinam* by John Greenwood (figure 1.4) at the St. Louis Art Museum. Here are some responses groups gave, and what they suggested about the observer:

- People are drinking and having a party (sees big picture).
- Triangles and vertical lines (sees shapes and composition).
- A man petting a dog, men dancing, a man getting sick (sees people and interaction or sees story details).
- There are three groups of people, or there are twenty-three people, twelve chairs, two tables (sees numerical relations).

1.4 Greenwood, John, *Sea Captains Carousing at Surinam*, 1758, oil on bed ticking, 37¾ × 75¼ in (95.9 × 191.1 cm), Courtesy of The St. Louis Art Museum. Photograph and digital image © 1997

- There are men in tricorn hats from the eighteenth century and native servants (sees historical aspect).

Pointing out the variety of responses to the group helps them understand that there are many ways to see and much can be learned by discussing the picture together.

DESCRIPTION VERSUS INTERPRETATION

It is important to distinguish between fact and interpretation. Most of the interesting points to discuss or write about a work will be interpretive. That is, they are open to question. For example, consider Chuck Close's painting *Fanny/Fingerpainting* (figure 1.5). The basic facts about this picture are as follows: It is a portrait, more than life-size, of an older woman. The artist painted it with fingerprints, based on a photograph. Interpretive issues are *opinions* as to whether or not she looks happy, or what the effect of this medium is. Both art and literature are open to interpretation; interpretations are defended based on a reading of the

1.5 Close, Chuck, *Fanny/Fingerpainting*, 1985, oil on canvas, 2.591 × 2.134 × .063 (102 × 84 × 2½), Gift of Lila Acheson Wallace, Photograph © 2001 Board of Trustees, National Gallery of Art, Washington D.C.

work. This is not to say that interpretation is any less valuable than fact; without it, we would not need to teach about art and literature! Interpretation is the effort to analyze and understand our own response to the work and to give voice to its meaning. It's especially important to ask students to explain their interpretations based on what they see.

FINDING THE IMAGE

Sometimes ideas and images change in the process of writing. The first words written about a work of art might contain many images. To help students refine their images, try an exercise called "center of gravity writing" as described by writer and educator Wendy Bishop.[1] Write for a few minutes in a stream of consciousness fashion, then circle the most important idea; write about that idea freely for a few minutes, then circle the most important idea. Continue to narrow the focus and refine the image.

Using small sheets of paper, write down as many words or short phrases that describe the image and your emotional response to it as possible in a five-minute time period. Each sheet should contain no more than three words. When time is called, arrange your sheets in the form of a poem, selecting and eliminating words that best emphasize your interpretation of the work. Here are two such forms based on Georgia O'Keeffe's *Ladder to the Moon* (figure 1.6):

Wind blows free
Dancing, jumping
Around the world
Breathing in
Floating free
Touching my soul
All of me
Letting go
Half a moon
No land below
Flying free
Climbing soul.

~DANA FARMER

1.6 O'Keeffe, Georgia, *Ladder to the Moon*, 1958, Collection Emily Fisher Landau, New York

Moon, Ladder, Mountains
Alone
Moons eye view, blue haze
Eerie night glow
To the heaven
Feeling heaven
Climb high
No fear
Pathway to happiness

~MARSHA STANLEY

NOTE

1. Wendy Bishop, *Released into Language: Options for Teaching Creative Writing* (Urbana, Ill.: National Council of Teachers of English, 1990).

Sense Impressions
and Word Images

Both visual art and writing communicate experience through a wealth of sensory information. Images combine sensations into a whole experience. A landscape will suggest sounds, temperature, light, breezes; a still life will suggest tastes, smells, and textures. Paying close attention when describing these sensations in paintings will sharpen our observation in everyday life.

LOOKING FOR SOUNDS AND MOVEMENTS

Simonides of Ceos is credited as having said that painting is "mute poetry." This activity encourages students to observe closely and to connect with the sensual qualities in the picture by describing sounds and movements. An adult class at the J. Paul Getty Museum participated in this activity based on *Two Watermills and an Open Sluice* by Jacob van Ruisdael (figure 2.1). Some of their observations are used as examples of this exercise.

Ask students to look at the paintings and to make a list of sounds and movements. The sounds can be words they invent. An example of a list based on the van Ruisdael painting follows:

2.1 van Ruisdael, Jacob, *Two Watermills and an Open Sluice*, 1653, 26 × 33¼ in (66 × 84.5 cm), The J. Paul Getty Museum, Los Angeles

drop	sway	swat	glide	stand
clack	chirp	gurgle	flow	whistle
spinning	flutter	roll	bounce	silence
squeak	fall	flip	crackle	rumble
rattle	drop	jump	churn	
roar	bark	rustle	roar	
splash	shout	slam	flow	
bristle	jump	rattle	bounce	
flap	clap	cool	stop	

Then, referring to one work of art at a time, ask students to read their lists. Ask each student to choose one work in the list and to explain the visual impetus that caused him or her to "see" and therefore think of that sound or movement. You are taking the intuited, "gut" feeling and helping them translate it into meaning.

Compare the words with the painting, and discuss how the artist used visual clues to cause us to hear and feel these sounds and movements. At this point you may have to stretch the group a bit. Let's say the student has chosen the sound "whoosh." It might be hard for that student to describe the visual impetus. You want the student to be specific. He or she might say, "Oh, the lines." You need to qualify the response. Which lines? "The lines of the trees, and the people's clothing blowing in the wind." Ask: "Can you describe these lines more fully? Are they straight, jagged, or curved? Why?" Keep encouraging more specific responses. This will help the student to be aware that lines, colors, shapes, and arrangement of forms are expressing something. You want the student to be fully aware that he or she is reading and responding to a visual language.

Using their list of words, ask students to each write a paragraph related to the sense of movement in the work. The paragraph can be about anything, but should include some visual clues and descriptions. Share the results.

This exercise can follow the warm-up given in chapter 1, using the same artwork, or can be done separately, allowing students to try the warm-up on their own. It works particularly well with and is a good preliminary activity for teaching about futurism.

ADJECTIVES: TEXTURE

Adjectives are one of the most important writing tools. Pinpointing the precise word for an image helps to focus and refine the image. This activity helps writers to focus on the precise word that will "show, not tell."

Prepare a "surprise bag" full of small objects with different textures, such as rocks, sticks, glass, coins, bits of fabric and fur, flower petals, wood, and so forth. Choose a painting that depicts a lot of textures. Seventeenth-century Dutch artists were focused on describing the details of what they saw with exactitude, so a Dutch still-life interior scene or portrait would work well for this. See, for example, *Still Life with Lemons, Oranges, and Pomegranate* by Jacob van Hulsdonck (figure 2.2).

2.2 van Hulsdonck, Jacob, *Still Life with Lemons, Oranges, and Pomegranate*, c. 1620–1640, 42 × 49.5 cm (16½ × 19½ in), The J. Paul Getty Museum, Los Angeles

Ask students to choose an object from the bag without looking, and not to show it to the group. Without looking at the object, they should feel it and think of words to describe its texture. "My object is soft and almost like fur, with little bristly fibers going in one direction," was the description for a piece of imitation leopard-skin fabric. (I first saw this technique demonstrated by my colleague, Nancy Berry, and I extended it to writing.)

Then the students should each select an object in the painting with a similar texture and try to describe its textures using adjectives. For example, "The cut-velvet dress of the lady in the Eliasz portrait has a texture that is soft, plush, deep, inviting, velvety." Each student in turn shares his or her chosen object and describes a similar texture in the painting. Encourage them to think of more than one adjective.

PRECISION: REFINING ADJECTIVES

Next ask students to focus on one object in the painting they particularly like and make a list of adjectives that describe it; not just in terms of its textures, but also in terms of how it appeals to the senses. For example, in the painting *Still Life with Lemons, Oranges, and Pomegranate* (figure 2.2), some students doing this exercise described:

> the pomegranate seed: translucent, succulent, juicy, clear
> the flower bud: springing, nascent, bursting, pulsating, budding

Then students should refine their description, selecting words to create a phrase that best describes the object while considering how the words sound together and how clearly the phrase communicates the image. Say to the students: "Why did you pick the object you are writing about?" You want your listener to see the exact qualities that you did when they hear the phrase: translucent, juicy pomegranate seed . . . fresh, bursting blossom.

WORD PAIRS

The interplay of words and ideas is the basis of writing. In this exercise, you will ask students to create word pairs, then longer phrases based on colors. (This is really combining verbal images to match the visual.)

This activity works with any artwork that has expressive color. As part of your discussion of the work, ask students to find the strongest color in the work. For example, with red, try to describe that exact red. Is it the color of cranberries or stop signs or flames? Then brainstorm other types of red. Cherry red or black cherry red or autumn red or Pompeian red. Then use another painting and ask students to choose a color and describe it with word pairings. Try to emphasize expression. For example, soft pink, satiny pink, petal pink, creamy pink. Depending on the level of your students, you may want to begin by creating two lists of words to describe colors; one describing qualities such as muddy, electric, vibrating, calm, sharp, restful, icy, clear, burnished, smoky, dark, glowing, and one referring to objects that are that color, such as mustard, marigold, buttercup yellow; lettuce, fern, sea green; royal, midnight, robin's egg blue; wine, claret, ruby red; birch, snowy winter white; peach, shell, earlobe pink. Share the results.

COLOR PORTRAITS

Ask students to choose one painting and create phrases for each color in it. For example, for a (Cézanne) landscape: bottle green, spinach green, brick red, maize yellow, sandy brown, cool blue. Try reading the list of color phrases and seeing whether the others can guess which picture the student has described. An example of this exercise, based on *I Raro Te Oviri (Under the Pandanus)* (figure 2.3), is given here:

> cool purple, deep turquoise, shade green, hot black, lush green, sparkling white, earth brown, warm peach, flash yellow, crackling red.

> ~MARILYN THOMPSON

THINKING IN PHASES

This exercise builds on the color portraits exercise just completed. Ask students as a group to describe one painting or sculpture in terms of

2.3 Gauguin, Paul, *I Raro Te Oviri (Under the Pandanus)*, 1891, oil on canvas, 26½ × 35¾ in (67.31 × 90.81 cm), Dallas Museum of Art, Foundation for the Arts Collection, gift of the Adele R. Levy Fund, Inc., 1963.58 FA

phrases. They should move beyond color this time. Examples would include rolling tide, passing clouds, foaming crests, washed sands, and clearing sky. Then each student chooses a painting and, still thinking in phrases, makes a descriptive list and builds a paragraph from it.

TONE AND HANDLING

Writers use words the way an artist uses paint. The words chosen, by their length, meaning, sound, and the way they are combined, create a *tone* or expressive quality for the written work. In the same way, how artists handle paint creates tone in a work. The handling allows us kinesthetically to "feel" the artist painting. Consider these paintings: *Cathedral* by Jackson Pollock (figure 2.4), with its drips, arc, and swirls,

2.4 Pollock, Jackson, *Cathedral*, 1947, enamel and aluminum paint on canvas, 71½ × 35¹⁄₁₆ in (181.61 × 89.06 cm), Dallas Museum of Art, gift of Mr. and Mrs. Bernard H. Reis 1950.87 © 2001. The Pollock-Krasner Foundation / Artists Rights Society (ARS), New York

and the lunging, heavy brushstrokes of *Slate Cross* by Franz Kline (figure 2.5). Many who see these works will see only lines and feel that the work has no content. But by taking the time to look at the lines, how they were formed, what feelings they create in the viewer, we can begin to read the expression of these works. Compare the works in terms of these questions:

1. Describe the lines. For example, are they free and fluid, choppy or elegant, dramatic or quiet, calm or tense?
2. What tools do you think made the lines? Why?
3. How did the artist move when making these lines?

2.5 Kline, Franz, *Slate Cross*, 1961, oil on canvas, 111¼ × 79¼ in (282.57 × 201.29 cm), Dallas Museum of Art, gift of Mr. and Mrs. Algur H. Meadows and the Meadows Foundation, Inc. 1968.9, © 2001 The Franz Kline Estate / Artists Rights Society (ARS), New York

Then ask students to describe a neutral object from a work that can be described with line, such as a stream of water, describing it three different ways and trying to use words to imitate or reflect the handling of paint in the work. Students from a gallery workshop based on Pollock gave the following as examples:

There is nothing more refreshing than a clear mountain stream that forms as the snow begins to melt on warm spring afternoons as the sun hits those icy . . . ~DEBBIE KUSTER

Waterfall beginning at the crevice, cutting across the rocks, splashing, singing, roaring, down, down, The spray releases freely sending droplets in all directions. Showering, floating, energetic and happy.

Not seeing the pool, I ask does the spray continue, does it end? No, it remains as continuous as the flow, as eternal as the rocks, on and on, splashing, dinging, down, down ~MARILYN THOMPSON

It
Flips
And
Flops
I run my finger
Under
The stream
To
Drops
And feel
The silk
The soft
The flow
The weight
The stream
the comfort
Slow
The tap
That pours
Across

My toes
The tub the warm
The
Way
It
Goes
The
Flow

~KATHY WALSH-PIPER

In comparison, these were written based on the Kline:

Harsh reflections
Splash go away
Moving, taking, destroying
Get out of my way
I am grabbing onto everything
The stones under me tear my body
The anger grows
Twirling
Stopping
I am falling.

~AMY REED

A muddy stream is quickly rushing over sticks and debris. The stream
is shallow and water is flying everywhere while a big brown bear leaps
into it trying to capture a plump spotted trout. The trout's tail flutters
and flips the water all about as it tries to free itself from the clutches of
the sharp claws. ~MARI PAIGE HEBERT

RHYTHM

"The visual path your eye follows across, around, or through a composition is referred to as movements. Depending on the nature of the pattern
and the accent of repeated components, your eye will 'move' at different
rates with different accents and pauses. This particular pace combined

with the visual path of movement is termed rhythm. The rhythm may be bold and staccato, as in the installation, or it may be smooth and fluid."[1]

An artist creates rhythm by repeating an element of art in the work, so the similarity of colors or shapes or lines makes a pattern. We read this pattern with our kinesthetic sense, as a rhythm. It can be a regular, even beat, or a staccato, or a long flow.

Look at these two textiles: the Indian *Palampore* (or bedspread) (figure 2.6) has a fluid rhythm like a waltz or a ballad. The *mawa'* (a sacred textile from Indonesia) (figure 2.7) has a staccato rhythm. Find two

2.6 *Palampore*, bedspread, India, c. 1750, cotton, 128 × 104 in, Dallas Museum of Art, gift of Mrs. Addison L. Gardner, Jr. in Memory of Richard W. and Anna L. Sears and of Mr. and Mrs. Alfred L. Bromberg in memory of Mr. and Mrs. I. G. Bromberg by exchange, 1992.9

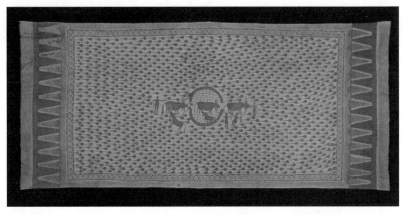

2.7 *Sacred textile (mawa'): tadpoles and water buffalo*, Indonesia, South Sulawesi, Ma'kale area, Sa'dan Toraja, early twentieth century, cotton, stamped, painted, 35 × 80¼ in, Dallas Museum of Art, the Steven G. Alpert Collection of Indonesian Textiles, gift of the McDermott Foundation, 1983.116

works with different rhythms and ask students: "What rhythm do you see? Steady or erratic? Fast or slow?" Tell the students to create a word poem in the shape of the square, using repeated words or sounds to create a rhythm or sound similar to that which they sense in the work. Think of short lines and phases as shapes; for the same length make a "square." Think of words and syllables as sound units. Then share results and guess which work matches the poems.

RHYTHM AS A PART OF MEANING

The artist Willie Cole uses equipment related to ironing, including ironing boards, as his art medium. His creative combination and deconstruction of these shapes and forms causes us to read them not as household tools, but as pure forms. The shape of the plate of the iron, for example, resembles faces, shields, African masks. This is called a visual pun. By repeating these shapes in a rhythmic pattern, he asks us to look at the shapes in a new way, to see it more than once. His art is also about transformation; the ironing board is transformed from the everyday object to one that should be considered for itself; its texture and patina are the sculptural material. Based on Cole's work, *Household*

Cosmology (figure 2.8), write a poem wherein a rhyming word creates the pattern, for example:

Iron, anger, passion, fire,
the heat, the fire,
a force entire.

A TASTE FOR ART

Some of the most sensuous works of art use paint or pastel to depict beautiful flowers, fruit, flesh, or food. Julie Springer at the National Gallery of Art created this idea for an alphabet poem. Try looking at a work of art with food, such as Bosschaert's *Flower Still Life* or Wayne Thiebaud's *Cakes* (figure 2.9), and write an alphabet poem that emphasizes the sensation of taste. Julie's start of such a poem, based on Thiebaud's work, is given here:

2.8 Cole, Willie, *Household Cosmology*, 1992, scorched ironing boards, wood, metal, 126 × 126 × 126 in (320.04 × 324.04 × 320.04 cm), Dallas Museum of Art, gift of The 500, Inc., 1996.71.A-F

2.9 Thiebaud, Wayne, *Cakes*, 1963, oil on canvas, 1.524 × 1.829 (60 × 72), Gift in Honor of the 50th Anniversary of the National Gallery of Art from the Collectors Committee, the 50th Anniversary Gift Committee, and the Circle, with Additional Support from the Abrams Family in Memory of Harry N. Abrams, Photograph © 2001 Board of Trustees, National Gallery of Art, Washington D.C. © Wayne Thiebaud/ Licensed By VAGA, New York, NY

All buttery confections,
Delicious edible fantasies,
Graceful honed icings join . . .

NIGHT LIGHT

The visual sensation of light is actually what allows us to see objects. Variations in light change the way we see color and also affect the mood or atmosphere of a painting. Some of the most interesting effects occur when light is very subtle, or minimal. We think of nighttime as a time of darkness, but if there were no light, we couldn't see at all! Try looking at

EDVARD MUNCH'S *STARRY NIGHT*
IN PAINTING AND PROSE POEM

Edvard Munch, a late nineteenth-century Scandinavian artist, believed strongly in the correspondence between art and writing. "All in all, art results from man's desire to communicate with his fellows. All methods are equally effective. Both in literature and in painting the technique varies according to the aims of the artist."[2] He was influenced by the symbolism movement in both art and poetry and by his poet friend August Strindberg. Munch wrote this prose poem based on memories of a star-crossed love affair and later painted the same image in his painting *Starry Night* (figure 2.10). The shifting images of land, sea, and sky, and especially the sky with the rising star, Venus, present a template for the viewer's interpretation. "Whether a picture resembles nature or not is irrelevant; a picture cannot be explained. The reason for its being painted in the first place was that the artist could find no other means for expressing what he saw."[3]

"Night Light" Prose Poem for *Starry Night*
written by the artist Edvard Munch

They walked across the floor to the open window leaning out looking down in that garden. It was chilly out there—The trees stood like big dark masses against the air.

It was too lovely—look there. She pointed along the water between the trees. Oh and up there is the moon—one is barely aware of it—it will emerge later I am so fond of the darkness— I cannot stand the light—it ought to be just like this evening when the moon is behind the clouds—it is so mysterious—The light is so indiscreet

It is like this with me she said after a while—on evenings like this I could do anything—something terribly wrong. Her eyes were big and veiled in the twilight . . .

It was as if she meant something with it—he had a premonition that something was going to happen—.[4]

a room in daylight, low light, and then semidarkness. How does the color change? Consider three different views of night, such as Corot's *Landscape with Lake and Boatman* (figure 2.11), Friedrich's *A Walk at Dusk* (figure 2.12), and Munch's *Starry Night* (figure 2.10). Each painting gives a very different interpretation of landscape at night. Write a short rhyming poem about the image of night as you read it in one of these works.

COMBINED SENSATIONS

Synesthesia refers to an ability to relate one sense to another. It can be a literary device, as when we refer to a bittersweet expression, a sour note, or a "juicy" green, or when we speak of a "sharp taste" or a "warm color."

2.10 Munch, Edvard, *Starry Night*, 1893, 53⅜ × 55⅛ in (135 × 140 cm), The J. Paul Getty Museum, Los Angeles

2.11 Corot, Jean-Baptiste-Camille, *Landscape with Lake and Boatman*, 1839, 24⅝ × 40½ in (62.5 × 102.2 cm), The J. Paul Getty Museum, Los Angeles

2.12 Friedrich, Caspar David, *A Walk at Dusk*, c. 1830–1835, 13⅛ × 17³⁄₁₆ in (33.3 × 43.7 cm), The J. Paul Getty Museum, Los Angeles

The artist Wassily Kandinsky had a special awareness of, and sensitivity to, a resonance of sense impressions and wrote about it in his theoretical art writing. Brainstorm with the group and make a list of expressions that are examples of synesthesia, such as "blue note."

Look at Kandinsky's painting *Improvisation 30 (Cannons)* (figure 2.13) and write a paragraph about the shapes and colors in the painting, describing them in terms of sounds or resonance. Then read how Kandinsky himself explained this painting in his book *On the Spiritual in Art*.[5]

2.13 Kandinsky, Wassily, *Improvisation 30 (Cannons)*, 1913, oil on canvas, 109.8 × 111 cm, Arthur Jerome Eddy Memorial Collection, 1931.511, The Art Institute of Chicago. All Rights Reserved. © 2001 Artists Rights Society (ARS), New York/SIAE, Rome, digital file © The Art Institute of Chicago. All Rights Reserved

For some writers and artists, such as Charles-Pierre Baudelaire and Kandinsky, synesthesia is the way they experience reality. Baudelaire explained his theory of correspondences as:

> It is not only in dreams, or in that mild delirium that precedes sleep, but it is even awakened when I hear music—that perception of an analogy and an intimate connection between colours, sounds, and perfumes. It seems to me that one and the same ray of light created all these things, and that their combination must result in a wonderful concert of harmony. The smell of red and brown marigolds above all produce a magical effect on my being. It makes me fall into a deep reverie, in which I seem to hear the solemn, deep tones of the oboes in the distance.[6]

Modern scientists have discovered that these sense experiences are connected in the limbic brain. For most people, these combined experiences are "sorted" or blocked by the brain. But for these artists—and 1 in every 25,000 people—these combined sensations are the way they experience reality. "Synesthesia also appears to run in families, leading some researchers to believe it has a genetic basis. Certain, many synesthetes report that a family member shared their ability. The writer Vladimir Nabokov, for example, wrote that as a young child, he informed his mother that the painted colors on his wooden alphabet blocks were 'all wrong.' She understood immediately, Nabokov recalled, because she, too, saw each letter in a distinctive hue."[7]

MUSICAL INSPIRATION

Explore the synergy between art forms by listening to music while looking at Georgia O'Keeffe's *Red Canna* (figure 2.14). While listening to the rhythm of the music, consider the visual rhythms and color notes O'Keeffe presents. Using the music and image as inspiration, create a short poem that reflects these ideas. Consider developing rhythmic patterns of speech using devices such as alliteration or clustering. Or, as an alternative exercise, you may consider playing upon the idea of stream of consciousness in your writing, letting the music carry your thoughts with it, as a type of free writing. An example of this exercise based on O'Keeffe's *Red Canna* is presented here:

2.14 O'Keeffe, Georgia, *Red Canna*, c. 1923, oil on canvas mounted in masonite, 36 × 29⅞ in (91.4 × 76.0 cm), Collection of the University of Arizona Museum of Art, Tucson, Gift of Oliver James

Abstraction so close up—one is immersed
reds swelling from whites to pinks soft velvet reds
bleed into liquid rubies teasing like a swirling
skirt softly blowing in the
breeze—morning sunlight looking
through the vibrant blood
of life awakening the
morning light sun parting
vibrations of pounding hearts

softening the
learning daily life. With best wishes. Cool violet strings of comfort
that come to the depths of
breathing with the glow of passion—the hope of fullness of the day.

~ELIZABETH HYDE

NOTES

1. Richard Pumphrey, *Elements of Art* (Upper Saddle River, N.J.: Prentice-Hall, 1996), 79.

2. See Louise Lippincott, *Edvard Munch: Starry Night* (Los Angeles, Calif.: J. Paul Getty Museum, 1988), 10.

3. Lippincott, *Edvard Munch*, 10.

4. Lippincott, *Edvard Munch*, 19.

5. See Wassily Kandinsky, *On the Spiritual in Art* (New York: Solomon R. Guggenheim Foundation, for the Museum of Non-Objective Painting, 1946).

6. Bettina L. Knapp, *Work, Image, Psyche* (Tuscaloosa: University of Alabama Press, 1985), 31

7. Quoted in Erica Goode, "When People See a Sound and Hear a Color," *New York Times on the Web*, www.nytimes.com, 1999 [accessed 30 March 2001]; also see Ann Kellan, "Ever Taste a Shape, or Smell a Color? Neurologist Explores Strange World of Synesthesia," www.cnn.com [accessed 30 March 2001].

Using Paintings to Write about the Setting: Landscape

Artists in landscape paintings lovingly capture the outdoors. In the past, the artist's record was the only means for holding the visual record of a place. Today, we also see many kinds of landscape through photographs and film. All of these can help us to see the use of landscape as symbolic and expressive, and how artists' choices create an image.

Artists interpret the land as sublime or threatening, wild or inviting, intimate or vast. Artists create expression by their choice of subject, colors, point of view, and treatment. In a similar way, writers can express their vision through deception, focus, point of view, and description. The setting sets the stage for a story by describing time and place.

Depending on the focus of a piece of writing, the setting can be a mere suggestion or the main subject. The same is true in painting. Landscape can be the background for the Mona Lisa or it can be the subject itself.

LANDSCAPE SETTINGS: WARM-UP VISUALIZATION

A good warm-up for thinking about landscape is to ask students to write about a particular landscape from memory, as an "I remember" poem. Ask students to recall in writing either a landscape they have seen in person or a landscape image from a book or a movie and to describe how that landscape affected him or her. Ask students to focus on the sensations and qualities that made it memorable: sights, sounds, smells, temperature, weather, and so forth. Share the results. If they are recalling a work of art, how was the image created? Have them describe the sensual details, sounds, or adjectives as they remember them. Discuss with students why they liked the image and what made it memorable. Ask: "How did you feel? What created that expression? Have you fully captured that in what you have written?"

This exercise may motivate students to learn about landscape traditions, their meanings, and style, and this can be a good introduction to nineteenth-century landscape traditions.

OBSERVATION AND SKETCHING

In the late nineteenth century, landscape was a popular subject both in America and in Europe. French artists in the forest of Fontainebleau and landscape painters in the American West created sketches out-of-doors, "*en pleine air*," as a memory aid. Back in the studio, the artist could re-create the scene from sketches and alter it for expressive purposes. Eventually, the sketch itself came to be valued as a work of art. Similarly, a writer may take notes about a setting or scene "on the spot," then use those notes later to write a complete description.

Consider a painting with a detailed setting such as *Forum, Pompeii, with Vesuvius in the Distance* by Christen Købke (figure 3.1) from the J. Paul Getty Museum. This painting was created shortly after Pompeii had been discovered. Photography had not yet been discovered. The artist traveled to Pompeii and made many sketches of the archaeological site, then from the sketches created this painting back in the studio. Discuss with students what kind of sketches the artist might have made to record the scene.

With the class, listen to detailed descriptions of places, such as those used for public radio broadcasts. Then ask students to create a word sketch focusing on one aspect of the painting, as if they were going to write a "radio sketch" describing it. Share results and see if you can, as a group, create a "word picture" that describes the scene from the various sketches. Here are some students' examples of these "sketches":

3.1 Købke, Christen Schjellerup, *Forum, Pompeii, with Vesuvius in the Distance*, 1841, 27⅞ × 34⅝ (68.5 × 86.3 cm), The J. Paul Getty Museum, Los Angeles

Two Corinthian capitals and part of their fluted columns appear today as large stumps that are just sitting on the ground, flat and solid against the ground. With the taller capital ever so gently leaning against the smaller one. They sit patiently amongst sparse shrubbery. ～NAOMI YAMADA

The ground is really dry; foliage has been picked over or probably eaten. Goats are grazing and foraging. There are patches where no foliage is growing at all; the earth has cracked from the dryness. Probably it has not rained for a while, almost desert-like. Lizards enjoy the hot arid soil. The ground is reddish in color. ～TOBEY SCHREIBER

The magnitude of this newfound site is outstanding. The multitude of columns seems to point out the architectural complexity of the site. These columns must have supported many temples and palaces. Many of which are scattered in broken piles throughout the site. ～LEONARD BRAVO

The magnificent ruins of the forum in Pompeii are a testimony of the danger of living in the proximity of a volcano. The massive mountain imposes itself in the background. The ruins of the forum are mainly shown with natural growth, weeds and a dirt road along the side. ∼LAURA GAVILAN-LEWIS

These descriptions were rearranged to create this description:

The magnificent ruins of the forum in Pompeii are a testimony to the danger of living in the proximity of a volcano. The magnitude of this newfound site is outstanding. The multitude of columns points out the architectural complexity of the site. These columns, many of which are scattered in broken piles throughout the site, supported many temples and palaces. Two Corinthian capitals and part of their fluted column appear today as large stumps that are flat and solid against the ground, with the taller capital gently leaning against the smaller one. They sit patiently amongst the sparse shrubbery. The massive mountain imposes itself in the background. ∼Written by gallery teachers at the J. PAUL GETTY MUSEUM

3.2 Church, Frederic Edwin, *The Icebergs*, 1861, oil on canvas, 64⅜ × 112½ in (163.51 × 285.75 cm), Dallas Museum of Art, anonymous gift, 1979.28

American art curator Eleanor Jones Harvey, in her exhibition *The Painted Sketch*, offered a new examination of the importance of the sketch. For nineteenth-century artists painting the landscape, there were several traditional kinds of sketches, such as:

croquis: a rapid thumbnail sketch, using just a few lines;

equisse: a preliminary sketch to flesh out the croquis;

pochade: a sketch concentrating on the range of light, color, or effect of a composition—larger issues of the picture;

study: a detailed drawing of one isolated aspect of nature, such as clouds or trees, which could be used directly in the final painting.

These sketches, or observations, were often painted outdoors and brought back to the artist's studio where they were integrated into the final work of art.[1]

3.3 Church, Frederic Edwin, *Off Iceberg, Newfoundland*, 1859, oil, possibly traces of graphite on thin board, $4^{15}/_{16} \times 11^{1}/_{8}$ in (124 × 283 mm), Cooper-Hewitt, National Design Museum, Smithsonian Institution/Art Resource, NY. Photo: Matt Flynn

3.4 Church, Frederic Edwin, *Floating Iceberg*, 1859, graphite and oil on board, 7½ × 14⅞ in (190 × 377 mm), Cooper-Hewitt, National Design Museum, Smithsonian Institution/Art Resource, NY. Photo: Matt Flynn

AN ARTIST'S USE OF ILLUSTRATION

Frederick Church (1826–1900) was an artist who explored the continents of America, both North and South, for awe-inspiring scenes. For his majestic painting *The Icebergs* (figure 3.2), he traveled to Labrador aboard ship and drew several sketches (*Off Iceberg, Newfoundland,* June 1859 [figure 3.3], *Floating Iceberg,* June or July 1859 [figure 3.4], *Iceberg, Newfoundland,* June or July 1859 [figure 3.5]) to create an image in his memory. Several sketches include atmosphere and color. Notice how each of these sketches focuses on a specific aspect of the scene: solid forms of the icebergs, its scale, the power of the sea, the atmosphere, and light. Consider how the awe-inspiring final work is different from the sketches in its complexity and expression.[2]

3.5 Church, Frederic Edwin, *Iceberg, Newfoundland*, 1859, oil, traces of graphite on thin board, $5\frac{3}{8} \times 14\frac{7}{8}$ in (135×353 mm), Cooper-Hewitt, National Design Museum, Smithsonian Institution/Art Resource, NY. Photo: Matt Flynn

ARTIST EXPLORERS

It is difficult for students today to imagine the "untamed wilderness" that was America in the age of exploration. Of course, there are many political and social issues involved in the history of that period, apart from the landscape. One of the most stunning events in our history was the meeting of disparate cultures and the exploration of the "new land."

American artists began painting landscapes in a more interpretive way in the early 1800s beginning with the Hudson River School artists. They believed that America was a new Eden. They were painting at a time when steamboats first allowed travel up the Hudson River. But soon landscape artists branched out to explore Labrador, South America, and the American west, encountering wonders such as icebergs, volcanoes, and vast prairies.

Imagine their encounters with unknown lands. Artists such as George Catlin (1796–1872) traveled with expeditions to the American West and painted the Native Americans. Catlin captured on canvas the Indians' ceremonies, hunting, games, and remarkable portraits, as well as a sense of the place of these peoples in the landscape. For example, Catlin both painted (*Prairie Meadows Burning* [figure 3.6]) and wrote about a tremendous prairie fire in Missouri:

3.6 Catlin, George, *Prairie Meadows Burning*, 1861–1869, oil on card mounted on paperboard, 465 × .625 (18⅜ × 24⅝), Paul Mellon collection, Photograph © 2001 Board of Trustees, National Gallery of Art, Washington D.C.

Our horses were swift, and we struggled hard, yet hope was feeble, for the bluff was yet *blue*, and nature nearly exhausted. . . . Not daring to look back, we strained every nerve. The roar of a distant cataract seemed gradually advancing on us—the winds increased, the howling tempest was maddening behind us—and the swift-winged *beetle* and *heath hens*, instinctively drew their straight lines over our heads. The fleet-bounding antelope passed us also; and the *still swifter* long-legged hare, which leaves but a shadow as he flies! Here was no time for thought—but I recollect the heavens were overcast—the distant thunder was heard—the lightning's glare was reddening the scene—and the smell that came on the winds struck terror to my soul![3]

Ask students to choose a feature in the local region and imagine how it once was. Write a description of a "first encounter" with the land. Or, conversely, study Catlin's Indian portraits such as *The White Cloud, Head Chief of the Iowas* (figure 3.7) and write about meeting a new culture.

3.7 Catlin, George, *The White Cloud, Head Chief of the Iowas*, 1844–1845, oil on canvas, 710 × .580 (28 × 22⅞), Paul Mellon collection, Photograph © 2001 Board of Trustees, National Gallery of Art, Washington D.C.

LANDSCAPE CLOSE-UP: JOHN JAMES AUDUBON

Landscape can lend itself to grand panoramas or intimate observation. The art of John James Audubon (1785–1851) can give us an appreciation of the wondrous details and variety in nature, as well as a new understanding of the fragile balance of the environment.

Audubon traveled the North American continent in the early 1800s to record the various species of birds and their habits and habitats in the New World. *The Birds of America* is a large folio of brilliant prints based on his drawings and watercolors done in the wild. Audubon's genius as an artist captured the bird's particular qualities of movement, and he arranged the bird in a characteristic natural setting, with a beautiful sense of design and color.

3.8 Audubon, John James, *Passenger Pigeon*, 1824, watercolor, gouche, and graphite, 26⅜ × 18¼ in, Collection of The New York Historical Society

3.9 Audubon, John James, *Carolina Parrot*, 1827–1838, hand-colored engraving, 33 × 23½ in (83.9 × 59.7 cm), North Carolina Museum of Art, Raleigh, Transfer from the North Carolina State Library

Although Audubon's works look as though he just came upon the bird in a bramble, he actually studied the birds carefully, knew what they ate, how they lived, and each detail of the ecosystem they lived within. To study them more closely, he killed birds and wired them in natural attitudes. His resultant works are carefully composed and wonderfully expressive.

Audubon also kept a journal to record his discoveries. Many of the species he saw in such abundance and wrote about are extinct now, such as the *Passenger Pigeon* (figure 3.8) and the *Carolina Parrot* (figure 3.9). Here's how he saw them:

> About the third day out we entered Cash Creek, a very small stream. Here I met a French artist, Jules De Mun, also bound for St. Genevieve. We learned that the Mississippi was covered by thick ice and impossible to ascent. Cash Creek (now the flourishing town of Trinity), located about six miles above the confluence of the Ohio and Mississippi, flows from some hills (north of its mouth) which are covered with oak, sumac and locust. Between it and the junction are walnut, ash and pecan in rich alluvial soil, along with some tangled cane and nettles. Now high, it abounded in fish and attracted innumerable Ducks driven south by winter from the Polar regions. The large sycamores contrasted with the cane beneath them. Thousands of Carolina Parrots roosted in their trunks. About fifty Shawanee Indian families camped here to harvest the pecans, and hunt Deer, Bear and Raccoon. . . .
>
> In passing over the Kentucky Barrens about twelve miles from Henderson, during autumn, I saw Passenger Pigeons flying southwest in greater numbers than, I thought, I had ever seen before. I dismounted, sat on a knoll, and began to count the flocks that might pass within reach of my eye in one hour. But the birds poured onward in such multitudes that I rose, discouraged, after having recorded 163 flocks in twenty-one minutes. The farther I proceeded the more I met. The air was literally filled with Pigeons that obscured the light of noonday like an eclipse. Dung fell, there and there, like melting snowflakes. The buzzing of wings had a curiously lulling effect on my senses. . . .
>
> I cannot describe to you the extreme beauty of their aerial evolution when a Hawk happened to press upon the rear of a flock. All at once—like a torrent—and with a noise like thunder—they rushed together to form a

compact mass. These almost solid masses of Pigeons darted forward in undulating and angular lines, descended and swept close over the earth with inconceivable velocity, mounted perpendicularly in such a way as to resemble a vast column, and, when high, wheeled and twisted within their unbroken lines that presently resembled the coils of a gigantic serpent.[4]

Have students write their own journal entry about a bird or animal, its habitat, its special quirks, and personality. Describe its movements, its beauty. Describe the plants of the environment where it lives. Write a description that shows the animal in its environment. (Suggest that students also use sketches to record their observations.)

ABSTRACT ART AS LANDSCAPE

Select abstract works that could suggest a landscape. This activity works particularly well with Mark Rothko's (1903–1970) works (e.g., figure 1.2). Abstract artists use line and color to express an idea. Their works are not literally a picture of a landscape, but rather can serve as a metaphor for the experience.

Select several abstract paintings and ask students to choose one painting from the assigned group to focus on. Ask students to imagine themselves in the landscape, with its sights, sounds, smells, temperature, and atmosphere. Ask students to write a description of the landscape. Allow at least ten minutes. Read the descriptions aloud to share results. Discuss the visual impetus for each interpretation.

POINT OF VIEW: THE ARTIST'S EYE

Both artists and writers have a "point of view" in observing their subjects. We hear the artist's voice through our eyes. "Look at this. . . ." Compare the two paintings given as examples of a rainy day by Gustave Caillebotte (*Rue de Paris: Temps de pluie* [figure 3.10]; *L'Yerres*, [figure 3.11]). Ask the students in which painting the artist is talking in first person. In third person? What is the difference in the tone and handling? Both paintings are about the experience of what one can see on a rainy day. But by focusing on the raindrops falling on water, without what art historians call the "narrative content" of showing people walking down the street, he puts us in his

3.10 Caillebotte, Gustave, *Rue de Paris, Temps de Pluie*, 1886, oil on canvas, 212.2 × 276.2 cm. Charles H. and Mary F. S. Worcester collection, 1964.336. The Art Institute of Chicago. All Rights Reserved, digital file © The Art Institute of Chicago. All Rights Reserved

place in a very personal moment. By comparison, the street scene is a more impersonal view, although still closely observed. The artist is describing a scene of two people walking down the street, based on his study of wide-angle photography, perspective, and the effects of light. Despite its careful construction, it appears to be a very "objective" painting. Have the students write a paragraph that starts with "It was raining . . ." about each picture. Encourage them to imitate the artist's point of view in each picture.

INTERIOR MONOLOGUE: MONET

For writers, the voice telling the story is usually a narrative or third-person point of view. This narrator can be an impartial observer describing people and events, or an all-knowing observer who knows the subjects' thoughts. Ask students to consider an impressionist painting and to describe in the third person what they see. Then explain the inten-

3.11 Caillebotte, Gustave, *L'Yerres, Effet de Pluie*, 1875, oil on canvas, 31⅝ × 23¼ in (80.3 × 5931 cm), Indiana University Art Museum: Gift of Mrs. Nicholas H. Noyes © 2001 Indiana University Art Museum. Photography by: Michael Cavanagh, Kevin Montague

tions of these artists (see sidebar) and ask students to write about the painting in the first person, imagining themselves as the artists choosing the subject, observing the subject, and engaging in the action of painting the picture. Write a description of these processes from the point of view of the artist. Here is an example by a teacher writing at the National Gallery in Washington:

Monet—at the Seine, near Giverny [figure 3.12]

Moving stillness—reflections on the river rise toward light, recede toward shadow on each ripple / the upper image still in lucent air / the lower image undulant and flowing in the absorbing, reflecting water. / Water which holds the mirror image yet holds it not at all / moving

THE ARTIST'S INTENTIONS

In late nineteenth-century France, the impressionists developed a new style of painting. Rejecting the "accepted" subjects and methods of painting, they chose subjects from the everyday world and tried to paint modern life. They concentrated on the act of seeing, using light and color to describe the transitory nature of what we actually see with our eyes. They tried to paint the changes in color due to time of day or atmospheric changes. This was a very self-conscious form of art, focusing on seeing as an experience. The act of painting was also part of this experience, so their canvases let us see the artist at work in the brushstrokes and textures, focusing on light and color.

3.12 Monet, Claude, *The Seine at Giverny*, 1897, oil on canvas, .815 × 1.005 cm (32⅛ × 39½ in), Chester Dale Collection, Photograph © 2001 Board of Trustees, National Gallery of Art, Washington D.C.

past, changing, changing the unchanging image. / Solid, aged trees, themselves moving in the shifting breezes, each leaf tilting to accept the light and turning back to darker hues and then into a newer angle by the thousands . . . millions / a warm, endless shivering in the sunlight: firm against the flowing sky, firm against the steadfast land, firm against the river's flow, echoing the light to green to blue to green to light, passing and re-passing through the spectrum's lower arc; / I shall reflect the sky, the woods, the shore, the water and stopping it to motionlessness on my canvas, let it move forever. ~ED SUNDT

POINT OF VIEW—MAJOR AND MINOR CHARACTERS

Writers often use first-person narrative in their works. This style of writing has the character, whether major or minor, speak in his own voice, such as Ishmael, Huck Finn, or Pip. Select a picture with major and

3.13 Copley, John Singleton, *Watson and the Shark*, 1778, oil on canvas, 1.821 × 2.297 cm (71¾ × 90½ in), Ferdinand Lammot Belin Fund, Photograph © 2001 Board of Trustees National Gallery of Art, Washington D.C.

WATSON AND THE SHARK

Watson and the Shark (1778) depicts the climactic moment of a shark attack in Havana Harbor in 1749. Nine men in a small boat are struggling heroically to save a fourteen-year-old boy who was swimming in the harbor when a shark attacked. A story published at the time of the painting relates that the shark had already pulled young Watson below the water twice and taken his right foot. As he surfaces for the third time, his rescuers managed to harpoon the shark and save the victim, who would commission this painting almost thirty years later.

The painting is a great example of a visual narrative. The painting is especially remarkable because the artist, John Singleton Copley, was new to large-scale, storytelling pictures when he painted it. Copley was an extremely gifted American colonial portrait painter who had come to London in 1774 to learn this more complex genre. His skill in portraiture served him well in portraying the various characters' expressions, from the shocked victim to the horror, concern, and fierce struggle of the rescue party. By choosing the split second when the shark was close upon the sailor, Copley ensured maximum drama for the scene. A tight visual "story line" is contained in the triangular composition. Outstretched arms and poised harpoon capture the moment. There are several stories written this scene: What was each person thinking or feeling? What will happen? What were the dangers for those who sailed in the eighteenth century? Why would Watson, who was an orphan, have sought this life?

The history of the painting carries another level of storytelling. Working in London, Copley re-created Havana Harbor, which he had never seen, from prints, and borrowed the arrangements of figures and gestures from Renaissance and ancient art. Also, the boy who was attacked by the shark lived, and later in his life, commissioned the painting in 1778. He later became Lord Mayor of London and willed the painting to an orphanage to inspire young boys like himself.

minor characters, such as John Singleton Copley's *Watson and the Shark* (figure 3.13). Ask students to write about the scene from the point of view of Watson; of the man with the boat hook; of the observers on another boat.

NOTES

1. Eleanor Jones Harvey, *The Painted Sketch: American Impressions from Nature 1830–1880* (Dallas: Dallas Museum of Art, 1998).

2. Harvey, *The Painted Sketch*, 39.

3. See Joan Carpenter Troccoli, *First Artist of the West: George Catlin Painting and Watercolors* (Tulsa, Okla.: Gilcrease Museum, 1993), 87.

4. John James Audubon, *Audubon, by Himself*, ed. Alice Ford (Garden City, N.Y.: National History Press, 1969), 44–55, 70.

Correspondence between Writing and Art: Characters

CREATING A CHARACTER

To write a good story, the writer must create a believable character. The key is to show the character through description and dialogue, rather than simply describing him or her. In the same way, artists' portraits can tell us how a person looks, but the best portraits capture a spark of personality and show us a believable person. Discuss several portraits and look for how the artist reveals the person's character from the viewpoint of setting, gestures, facial expression, hands, choice of costume, and accessories.

PORTRAITS

Choose a portrait that has a strong presence or character. Ask students to pretend the sitter is a character in a play. Write the opening line to the play. Then ask students to imitate the body language of that person, to demonstrate that person in action, and to describe that person's next move. How will they get up from the chair? What gestures will they make? What will they do with their hands? Will they move quickly or slowly? Gracefully or awkwardly?

Now ask students to choose a portrait and write a paragraph that shows that figure in action and uses details from the picture to develop a written psychological portrait, including dialogue. Analyze how the person looks, moves, speaks, and how they relate to the objects in the setting. Be sure to include both positive and negative aspects of the person and to present a realistic view of the personality.

ARTISTIC EXAMPLES OF PORTRAITS

Over the centuries, artists have used portraits to commemorate, aggrandize, or leave a lasting record of an individual. Every figure in a particular work of art is not a portrait; in a portrait the artist tries to represent the person as well as the physical presence.

Jacques-Louis David's portrait of Napoleon (figure 4.1) stresses the heroic and grand aspects of his person and reflects his rank and importance more than his true personality. This painting uses both portraiture and symbolism to portray Napoleon as a political hero. Napoleon stands in his study, where he has worked all night. The candles are low and the clock reads 4:13. His sword and a scroll marked "code" reflect his achievements as a lawmaker and military leader, and he is dressed in the uniform of a colonel of the Forth Grenadiers of the Imperial Guard. Despite the formal setting, his posture is at ease, with the characteristic gesture of his hand resting in his vest. The artist has portrayed Napoleon as he would probably have liked to be remembered.

Compare this with Jean-Auguste-Dominique Ingres' portrait of the Marquis de Pastoret (figure 4.2). Although the uniform, pose, and trappings of rank are comparable, it is the haughty yet troubled face of the Marquis and the underlying tension in his svelte body, cocked elbow, and splayed hand that draw our attention. Ingres has created a psychological portrait of this complex man, who was embroiled in the politics of successive regimes in nineteenth-century France.

4.1 David, Jacques-Louis, *The Emperor Napoleon in His Study at the Tuileries*, 1812, oil on canvas, 2.039 × 1.251 cm (80¼ × 49¼ in), Samuel H. Kress Collection, Photograph © 2001 Board of Trustees, National Gallery of Art, Washington D.C.

CHARACTERS IN CONFLICT

One of the ways a writer creates a story is by introducing conflicts for the character. Conflict or tension in a character also creates drama in a work of art. Mankind can be seen in conflict with itself, with others, with nature, or even with the supernatural.

Consider Rodin's sculpture of Jean d'Aire, one of the *Burghers of Calais* (figure 4.3). This figure is a study for a group portrait that commemorates a historical event. In 1347, the burghers, or town leaders, of Calais gave themselves up as hostages to save their town, which was under

4.2 Ingres, Jean-Auguste-Dominique, *Amédée-David, The Marquis de Pastoret*, 1823–1826, oil on canvas, 103 × 83.5 cm, Estate of Dorothy Eckhart Williams; Robert Allerton, Bertha E. Brown and Major Acquisitions endowments, 1971.452, The Art Institute of Chicago. All Rights Reserved, digital file © The Art Institute of Chicago. All Rights Reserved

siege by the English. The group of hostages is depicted in a realistic manner, dressed in sackcloth and being led with ropes around their necks to surrender the key to their city. Jean d'Aire was supposed to be holding the key. Look at his grim, determined face and stance, his clenched fists. Rodin's figure has a psychological and emotional intensity that represents the real historical person, Jean d'Aire, even though he had no way of portraying a likeness.

Ask students to choose a hero from an event in history and create a written portrait of that hero at the moment of crisis, showing not only his appearance, but his emotions and actions. You may want to use an "epic" style, such as the examples of couplets given here:

Burghers of Calais

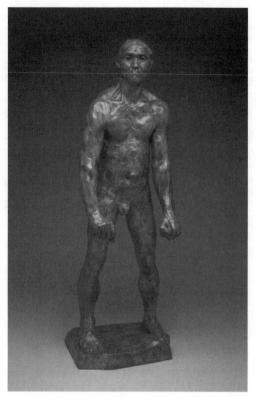

4.3 Rodin, Auguste, Jean d'Aire from *The Burghers of Calais*, 1886, bronze, 81 × 28 × 24 in, Dallas Museum of Art, given in memory of Louie N. Bromberg and Mina Bromberg by their sister Essie Bromberg Joseph, 1981.1

Annealed in the maker's fire, skin burnt black
on the naked bodies barely slung with sack
the muscles on their backs strain in Rodin's sun.
These men know what's left to be done.
The stakes of commerce animate eye and hand,
timeless wisdom lies heavy on each lined face,
the consequences clear in the way they stand
huddled and herded into the marketplace.
From the Strait of Dover, a North wind blows.
Fathers and husbands—six burghers of Calais—
simple rough men on their way to the gallows,

contemplating who will go first, what to say.
They are roped together, heart to hand to heart,
the power of character making beauty in art.

~RONALD THORPE

POINT OF VIEW—MONOLOGUE

A monologue is a first-person narrative that presents the thoughts of one character through conversation, often with a reflective and philosophical tone. Using the painting that shows a reflective (perhaps older) person, such as *Into the World There Came a Soul Called Ida* (figure 4.4), by Ivan Albright, have students create a monologue for the central figure that

4.4 Albright, Ivan, *Into the World There Came a Soul Called Ida*, 1929–1930, oil on canvas, 142.9 × 119.2 cm, Gift of Ivan Albright, 1977.34, © The Art Institute of Chicago, All Rights Reserved, digital file © The Art Institute of Chicago. All Rights Reserved

describes that individual's life, memories, joys, and regrets, and what that person sees in the mirror.

DIALOGUE

Writers use dialogue, or conversations between characters, to develop characters or to advance the plot of a story. When writing a dialogue, much is revealed by the diction and grammar, the tone of the characters, as well as by what they actually say. In a work of art, a conversation is sometimes implied. These writing activities focus on different aspects of dialogue.

Dialogue to Develop Plot

Paintings of everyday life such as Mary Cassatt's painting, *The Tea* (figure 4.5) often lend themselves to creating a dialogue. Cassatt was an American artist working in Paris. Like many impressionist artists she often

4.5 Cassatt, Mary, *The Tea*, 1879–1880, oil on canvas, $25\frac{1}{2} \times 36\frac{1}{4}$ in (64.8 × 92.1 cm), Courtesy, Museum of Fine Arts, Boston. Reproduced with permission. © 2000 Museum of Fine Arts, Boston. All Rights Reserved

painted scenes of leisure activities of the bourgeoisie. In particular, Cassatt's work portrayed the world of women of her own social class. This scene of an afternoon tea is one of relaxed elegance. The thoughtful figure at the left is the artist's older sister Lydia, whom she frequently painted.

Have students write a dialogue for these two ladies at tea. The way they speak should reflect their gentility and imply their character, but in this exercise, the writer should also focus on revealing the plot of a story through what they say. Are they discussing a play they have seen or analyzing a friend's behavior? Are they discussing the past or the future? Share results. Have the students listen to one another's dialogue and see if they can find a spot where having one character repeat the other's words would connect the conversation more clearly.

Dialogue about a Work of Art

Works of art engender conversation. Have students pretend they are eavesdropping in your local museum. Tell them to write a dialogue between two visitors about one work of art. Students will need to choose the work and define the characters. How old are they? What are their interests? How would they respond to the work and to each other? Share the results.

Poetic Dialogue Based on Burne-Jones

The Pilgrim at the Gate of Idleness by Sir Edward Coley Burne-Jones (figure 4.6) is based on Chaucer's poem "Romance of the Rose," which follows an allegorical journey. The pilgrim, searching for Virtue, meets a lovely young woman who represents Idleness. Conversation is implied by the arrangement of figures, their gestures, gaze, and stance. Ask students to create a poetic dialogue for the painting that reveals the pilgrim's temptation and struggle within himself. Some examples from students using this painting are given here:

> Come inside and stop your wander
> I must go on; I haven't been yonder
> You must stop this aimless path you go
> I must proceed for what I don't know

4.6 Burne-Jones, Sir Edward Coley, *The Pilgrim at the Gate of Idleness*, 1884, oil on canvas, 38 × 51½ in (96.52 × 130.81 cm), Dallas Museum of Art, Foundation for the Arts Collection, Mrs. John B. O'Hara Fund

To be content you should aspire
I have not found what I require
Take my hand and come inside
End your journey, in me confide.

~MARIE PAIGE HERBERT

Dear traveler, come hither and take your ease
I've waited here to do as you please
The road is long and my destination unknown
But I fear I can't heed your alluring tone
Ah, dear one, you have nothing to fear
Within these walls, all will be clear.

~MELINDA MAYER

Be still, and join me for a night

you must be weary from your flight.
Hush and do not tempt my will
For I have far to travel still
But the night is calling you to rest
Stay here and sleep upon my breast
I cannot stay, my feet be mired
I must not stay, though I am tired.

~MARILYN THOMPSON

Art Develops Imagination

Because artists create powerful images, they stimulate us to think about and see things in new ways, in clearer detail. The following activities all use the work of art as a prompt for imagination.

STORYTELLING: REWRITING A CLASSIC

Have you ever read a book, then seen a movie based on the book? Some aspects of the movie are bound to be different from the way you visualized them while reading. Whether a filmmaker or a painter, an artist takes a story and creates images for it. A film tells the whole story; a painting shows only one scene. To tell a story well, the painter must create very convincing characters, setting, and action. Many times the artist can assume that the viewer knows the story, and signs or symbols can represent previous and future events. Still, it is the believable and likable representation of character and setting that will make the story come alive.

Discuss the elements of a story—character, plot, description, and dialogue—with students. Then look at "narrative" paintings (paintings that depict an event in history or a story) together and discuss the limitations of visual art in telling a story. In a painting, an artist can only depict one moment in the story. On the other hand, the artist describes the scene in a vivid, imaginative way. Artists allude or give reference to other parts of the story, for example, a crown of thorns at the feet of the *Pieta* refers to earlier events.

Certain myths and legends have such universal appeal that they are retold time and time again, becoming classics. For example, the legend of St. George and the Dragon tells of a strong hero confronting a horrible dragon to save a beautiful princess, and has been the subject for artists for centuries. A few examples would be the work of Raphael, *Saint George and the Dragon* (figure 5.1) and Bernardo Martorell's *Saint George Killing the Dragon* (figure 5.2).

5.1 Raphael, *Saint George and the Dragon*, 1506, oil on panel, .533 × .476 × .085 (21 × 18¾ × 3¼), Andrew W. Mellon Collection, Photograph © 2001 Board of Trustees, National Gallery of Art, Washington D.C.

5.2 Martorell, Bernardo, *Saint George Killing the Dragon*, 1430–1435, tempera on panel, 155.3 × 98 cm, Gift of Mrs. Richard E. Danielson and Mrs. Chauncey McCormick, 1933.786, The Art Institute of Chicago. All Rights Reserved, digital file © The Art Institute of Chicago. All Rights Reserved

Have the students consider different versions of the story. The artists have visualized the essential characters and created their images, imagined a setting. Discuss how artists' interpretations of the hero and the dragon differ. What action in the story did they choose to portray—St. George encountering the dragon, the battle itself, or the victory? How did the artists use details to "show" us the story?

Students can rewrite the story of St. George (or another narrative) based on a painting. Add details such as how the dragon looked, how the people felt, what they wore, how St. George looked, and what were the sounds, smells, and textures in the story. Create a dialogue between the king, the princess, and St. George.

THE TALE OF ST. GEORGE

St. George epitomized the ideals of chivalry. He rescued the inhabitants of a town from a fierce dragon. The beast had demanded that the townspeople sacrifice their sheep, then their children. The king's daughter Cleodelinde would have been next. St. George killed the dragon with his spear and converted the town to Christianity. Ask: "Which moment in the story did these artists choose to portray? Which part of the story would you choose to illustrate—the battle with the dragon or the moment of triumph? Why?"

In this very detailed painting, *St. George Killing the Dragon*, the artist has managed to tell quite a bit of the story through details. The long road in the background tells us of St. George's journey, and the beautiful princess who was to be sacrificed is standing by a lamb. The grisly litter of skulls and bones at the dragon's feet makes the scaly dragon even more frightening. Opposite it is the beautiful white horse and St. George poised to strike—the cloak and banners with his coat-of-arms streaming behind him.

STORY COMPLETION

Artists often choose to depict the most dramatic moment in a story. In Frederic Remington's painting *The Advance Guard, or the Military Sacrifice* (figure 5.3), we see a scene from the days when the artist accompanied the U.S. Sixth Cavalry across the Badlands in pursuit of the Sioux Indians. The Advance Guard was the group of soldiers who went first, as a sentinel, to warn the troops of danger. Ask students: "What's happening in this picture? What will happen next?" Then tell students to write an ending for this story or to write a newspaper account of this event.

INVENTING SYMBOLS

Symbols are objects that act as signs to represent something else, such as an idea, a country, or a team. Artists use symbols to convey meaning in

5.3 Remington, Frederic, *The Advance Guard, or the Military Sacrifice*, 1890, oil on canvas, 34⅜ × 48½ in, The George F. Harding Collection, 1982.802, The Art Institute of Chicago. All Rights Reserved., digital file © The Art Institute of Chicago. All Rights Reserved

a work of art. For example, the painting *Ceres*, or an *Allegory of Summer* (figure 5.4), uses symbols to represent the season. This oval painting was created as one of four panels on *The Seasons* for the dining room of a French palace in the early eighteenth century. The lovely women in the picture herself is an allegory of summer. Fair and loosely robed, sitting on a cloud, wearing a crown of poppies, cornflowers, and wheat, she is the picture of warmth, indolence, and abundance. The scythe in her hand is a symbol of the harvest; the other figures refer to the summer zodiac signs—the twins for Gemini, crab for Cancer, and Leo the lion. The colors the artist chose—pink and gold—are warm and soft like the season. Unfortunately, the painting that represented Spring was destroyed in a fire and Autumn and Winter are missing. Have students choose one of the latter three "missing" seasons and write a description of a central figure and attributes that are symbols for the season. Have students tell what colors they chose and describe the panel in detail.

5.4 Watteau, Antoine, *Ceres (Summer)*, 1715–1716, oil on canvas, 1.416 × 1.160 (55¾ × 45⅝), Samuel H. Kress Collection, Photograph © 2001 Board of Trustees, National Gallery of Art, Washington D.C.

TIME CAPSULES

Many objects in an art museum are real time capsules because they actually came from another time and place. In some cases, they will be the only record of that time. Research can help us to learn more about the culture and history surrounding an object, but its real presence can help us to feel the past and to imagine the people who made and used it.

AN ARCHAEOLOGIST'S NOTES

Archaeologists study the past from objects (and objects from the past!). Clarence S. Fisher, an archaeologist from the University of Pennsylvania, excavated a golden figurine (figure 5.6) from an Egyptian tomb in 1916. Fisher kept very thorough records for his day, although they are still very summary by modern archaeological standards. He recorded all of the finds in the field register (figure 5.6), where he also included sketches of artifacts and transcriptions of hieroglyphic texts. The records include the location of the tomb in which the object was found, and sometimes the location within the tomb. They also give the location of the tomb within the cemetery, with a number that corresponds to a quadrant on one of his maps of the site. Many of the finds were also photographed in the field. In his diary, Fisher gives a daily account of his excavation matter-of-factly, not the sort of dramatic exclamations we are used to hearing in the movies or accounts of Howard Carter discovering the tomb of Tutankhamen. As deciphered from figure 5.5, this is how he describes the discovery of Sekhmet's statue:

> 10th of June 1916 Saturday
>
> Today was one of our banner days. Ganouy found a pocket on the North edge of this trench, near the axis of the building, which contained a quantity of gold and faience jewelry. The separate pieces were not in situ [in place] and mixed in debris. The level was about 100 meters below the level of earth left after the removal of the Ptolemaic walls by elkakheem. Period therefore just prior to 320 B.C. The main piece was a figurine of Sekhmet in solid gold 72 millimeters long. Then there was a small figure of Nefer-tem [figure 5.6] with small cylindrical headdress and holding a staff in both hands.[1]

Imagine the curiosity and excitement of opening this "time capsule." Have students write about this find in a more dramatic way, as if they were writing a movie script.

Archaeologists uncover wonderful treasures from many cultures. The gold headdress in figure 5.7 was found in Colombia and dates from 400–700 A.D. You can see two crocodiles' heads in profile and other

5.5 Fisher, Clarence S., 1916–1917, Diary: *Archaeologist's Note*, p. 142 (June 10, 1916). Memphis Expedition, University of Pennsylvania Museum Archives

5.6 *Necklace with Sekhmet Amulet*, Egypt, Dynasty 26, reign of Amasis, 570–526 B.C., gold and chalcedony, amulet, h. 7.6 cm (3 in), Coxe Expedition, 1916, 20-70-19, University of Pennsylvania Museum of Archaeology and Anthropology

5.7 *Headdress Ornament with Heads Flanked by Crested Crocodile*, Colombian, A.D. 400–700, gold, 10 × 11½ in, Dallas Museum of Art, The Nora and John Wise Collection, gift of Mr. and Mrs. Jake L. Hamon, the Eugene McDermott Family, Mr. and Mrs. Algur H. Meadows and the Meadows Foundation, and Mr. and Mrs. John D. Murchison, 1976.W.319

faces used to designate this spectacular piece. It was probably part of the ceremonial dress for an important person. Imagine seeing it move, jingle, and sparkle on a person's head. The person would have also been wearing gold bracelets, anklets, and ear and nose ornaments. No one knows for sure exactly when it was worn or by whom, so students can use their imagination to describe the event.

DREAMS AND FANTASY

Imagination is the creative engine of our minds that reforms objects and impressions sensed into something new. A fantasy is an invention of our minds; it could be a character, a place, an animal, or a way of life. Some fantasies are believable, close to reality; others are beyond reality or fantastic. Artist and writers use both kinds of fantasy in their work.

Dreams are the thoughts and images that occur when we are asleep. Dreams are different from waking thoughts—irrational, disordered, beyond conscience or time. A dream seems to "happen to us." Artworks appear "dream-like" when they juxtapose disparate elements.

For example, Giorgio de Chirico's painting *The Philosopher's Conquest* (figure 5.8) is hard to describe as a scene. It combines classical columns, a train, a clock, windows and doorways, a cannon, and artichokes! The odd juxtapositions and confused space create a sense of something unresolved and a mood of foreboding. Have students invent the story behind Chirico's painting, answering the logical questions who, what, when, where, and why for the illogical scene.

ASSOCIATION: CREATE A
UNIVERSE FROM FRAGMENTS

Joseph Cornell was an artist who enclosed small everyday objects within framed boxes to create works of art that are rich with metaphor. The method of combining everyday or "found" objects to make a picture is called collage; but Cornell's work is a particularly complex form of this medium. He lived outside New York City, and his life was limited by his responsibility to take care of his mother and sister. Forays into the city, to recharge his imagination by looking at store windows, theater signs, and hotel bills, were the source for his work. The objects chosen allow

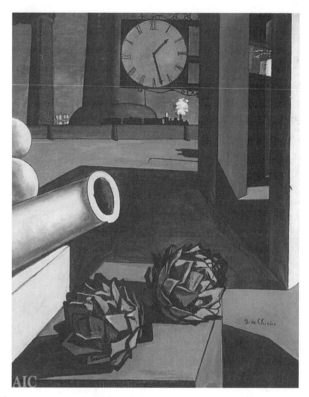

5.8 de Chirico, Giorgio, *The Philosopher's Conquest*, 1914, oil on canvas, 125.1 × 99.1 cm, Joseph Winterbotham Collection, 1939.405, The Art Institute of Chicago. All Rights Reserved. © 2001 Artists Rights Society (ARS), New York/ADAGP, Paris, digital file © The Art Institute of Chicago. All Rights Reserved

multiple and universal meanings. Their selection and arrangement creates new relationships, within a constraint of style that is taut and poetic.

Soap Bubble Set (*Ostend Hotel*) from circa 1958 (figure 5.9) is a good example. The objects included—glass dishes, a chart of the moon, a pipe, a doll's head, cups, an egg—all have circular elements.

For this activity have students create a list of associations for circles. Then have them create a list of relationships that the circles suggest and a list of associations for each object. If available, look at other Cornell boxes that contain words. How can words become part of the image? What is the effect?

5.9 Cornell, Joseph, *Soap Bubble Set (Ostend Hotel)*, 1958, oil on canvas, 15¾ × 14¼ in, The Wadsworth Atheneum Museum of Art, Hartford, Conn. Purchased through the gift of Henry Keney. © The Joseph and Robert Cornell Memorial Foundation / Licensed by VAGA, New York, NY

Now ask students to choose a "found object" and write a list of associations and a poem based on the list that connects the images on the list in some way and includes some "found words."

IF OBJECTS COULD TALK: MASKS

Some objects were created to take on a persona; they speak to us. The elaborate beaded mask and feathered hat shown in figure 5.10 were part of a set of ritual clothing created for the elephant masquerade of an African tribe. Dancers of the Bamelike people of the Cameroon Grasslands would wear these with blue and white tunics trimmed with monkey fur and long skirts that concealed their bodies. Dancing with rattles on their ankles

5.10a *Elephant Mask*, Africa, c. 1910–1930, palm-leaf fiber textile, cotton textile, glass beads, palm-leaf ribs, 58 × 26 × 6½ in (147.32 × 66.04 × 16.51 cm), Dallas Museum of Art, Textile Purchase Fund, 1991.54.1

5.10b *Hat for elephant mask*, Africa, c. 1910–1930, basketry, wood, feathers, cotton textile, 9¾ in (24.76 cm) diameter 32 in (81.28 cm), Dallas Museum of Art, Textile Purchase Fund, 1991.54.2

and holding a fly whisk, they represented the elephant as well as the king. The brilliant color and texture of the feathers and the vibrant patterns of the beaded "trunk" reflected the mighty power of both.

Ask students to imagine this heavy mask on their head, and move their head like an elephant, swinging the weight of the beaded "trunk," then to write as if they were the dancer/elephant/king. What proclamations would they make?

METAMORPHOSIS

The culture of the northwest coast Indians was based on myths that explained their worldview and their environment. Their totem poles and carved decorations represented the animal spirits that were heraldic symbols for the various clans of their social structure. For example, the symbol of the whale, raven, or walrus would represent a clan. It would also represent shared beliefs and stories about these spirits, who could exist in more than one life form. The totems also represented this metamorphosis in the formalized and spatially controlled forms, which merge into each other, just as the spirits can move from one life form to another. Thus, the raven, crouching figure, and frog on the walrus ivory knife handle in figure 5.11 are interconnected and emerge from one another. There were many stories and myths about these spirit creatures of the natural world. This retelling of one story about the raven spirit, "Box of Daylight" reflects its ability for metamorphosis:

> At the beginning of the world, it was dark. Some people had heard of daylight, but no one had seen it. Some people said that daylight was owned by the River Chief. One of the creatures who lived in this dark world was Raven. Raven was wise and greedy, sly and meddlesome and he could change his form whenever he wanted. Raven decided to find out about daylight. He changed himself into a hemlock needle and fell into a spring. When the chief's daughter came to drink, she swallowed him, and in time Raven was born as the River Chief's grandson. The River Chief doted on his grandson, even when this grandson threw tantrums. When Raven screamed, the River Chief let his grandson play with the Moon Box. Raven opened the box and the moon escaped into the sky. Raven screamed again and his grandfather let him play with the Box of Daylight. As soon as he received it, Raven changed from a boy to a raven

5.11 *Long-Beaked Bird with Crouching Figure and Masks*, Canada, nineteenth century, ivory, pearl shell, wood, $4\frac{1}{8} \times 1\frac{5}{8} \times 3\frac{13}{16}$ in (10.48 × 4.13 × 9.69 cm), Dallas Museum of Art, The Eugene and Margaret McDermott Art Fund, Inc., 1977.28.MCD

and disappeared into the darkness. Raven took the box to the people. He told them he had daylight and even allowed a few streaks to escape. But no one believed him. Raven grew angry and threw open the Box of Daylight, scorching his white feathers black. ~retelling by KEN KELSEY

Notice that this myth accounts for several natural phenomena—how the sun and moon came to be seen by man and why the ravens' feathers are black. Encourage students to create another tale of Raven that accounts for these phenomena.

NOTE

1. See *Diary of Clarence Fisher: Expedition Records* (Memphis: University of Pennsylvania Archives, 1917).

For Younger Students

As discussed in the introduction, exposure to visual imagery literally builds the imagination. It is especially important for younger children who are used to "reading" the world without words to learn to connect words and images. As the brain stores memories, dividing them into sense components, visual clues provide a powerful connector. Researcher Ilona Holland of the University of Delaware has documented that museum visits also improve vocabulary skills.[1] Until language skills mature to the point of writing paragraphs, teachers can prepare students for "reading" pictures through verbal, group writing, or completion activities.

DRAWING DISCUSSION FROM ART

Younger children (ages six to eight) are just learning to write, but they are very accustomed to relating pictures and stories from their exposure to artists' illustrations in picture books. Ask students to choose a favorite picture from a storybook. Why do they like the picture? How does having a picture affect how they listen to the story? Ask students to tell the story and explain why they like that picture. Ask questions about any details they haven't mentioned, such as "Why do you think the artist might have put that in the picture?" It's important for children to know that the artist created the picture from the way he or she imagined the story. Show them how to find the name of both author and illustrator. Ask if they would have changed anything in the picture.

When my third-grade students were learning to write stories, they often would write only one sentence. I found that asking them to draw a picture with the story and to tell about the picture helped them to keep writing and to create a fuller story.

TREASURE HUNT

To start connecting writing and art, create a "treasure hunt" game. Choose a variety of paintings, sculptures, or decorations the students will enjoy. Write a short, very simple rhyming poem describing each one in some aspect. Then ask the students to find a picture, matching it to the poem that will fit the "clue." For example:

Jump and Stop
A hop-scotch step
Along the path
What will come next?

Slip and slide
Catch a line
When you're sailing
The day is fine.

I see a steeple
Past fields and trees
The weather vane
Will catch the breeze.

Or read a story with a subject such as a dragon, a royal couple, or the Old West that could relate to several works of art. Then put up a "gallery" of several reproductions of paintings with related subjects and ask the students to choose the one they think relates to the story and explain why.

EXPERIENCE STORY

To encourage children to start writing early, share a work of art the children will enjoy, such as *Takenouchi no Sukune Meets the Dragon King of the Sea* (figure 6.1). This sculpture depicts the story of Takenouchi, a leg-

6.1 *Takenouchi no Sukune Meets the Dragon King of the Sea*, 1879–1881, bronze, 54 × 40 × 26 in (137.16 × 101.6 × 66.04 cm), Dallas Museum of Art, Foundation for the Arts Collection, The John R. Young Collection, gift of M. Frances and John F. Young, 1993.86.11FA

endary Japanese warrior-statesman who was believed to have lived for 360 years. Legend says Takenouchi dreamed that he was ordained to destroy a terrible sea monster. After the monster was slain, Ryu, the Dragon King of the Sea, and his servant came forth from the water to thank the hero and brought him a crystal ball and power over the seas.

First, look for details together. Then ask the students questions such as: "How can we tell Ryu and the servant came from the water? How are they different from the warrior? What do they bring him?" Have children work together to write the story of before and after this scene. Continue to encourage the students by asking questions like: "What did the sea monster look like? Was it a dragon, an octopus, a giant eel? Where was the battle? How did Takenouchi kill the monster? What will be his next challenge? What will the hero do with his new powers? What will he do with the crystal ball?" Encourage more than one answer to each question.

SENTENCE COMPLETION

Ask the students to complete sentences based on viewing a picture such as *The Eight Immortals of the Wine Cup* (figure 6.2). Some examples of starter sentences are listed here:

> I am standing . . .
> I can hear . . .
> The trees are . . .
> The water is . . .
> Close up I can see . . .
> Far away I can see . . .
> I see three people who are . . .

Exercise their imagination in the same way by focusing on a character. A list of starter sentences is provided here:

> This person is . . .
> The expression on the face is . . .
> This person lives . . .
> His/Her family is . . .
> He/She likes to . . .

6.2 *The Eight Immortals of the Wine Cup*, Japan, Momoyama period, c. 1600, ink, pigment on gold, one of a pair of six-fold screens, 65¾ × 20 × 13 in, Dallas Museum of Art, The Eugene and Margaret McDermott Art Fund, Inc., 1989.78.A-B/MCD [detail]

He/She worries about . . .
When I met this person . . .
He/She likes most to . . .

CIRCLE STORY

Select a painting the children can imagine stepping into, such as Rousseau's *The Waterfall* (figure 6.3) or Hendrick Avercamp's *Winter Landscape* (figure 6.4). Help students to imagine themselves in the picture by using sounds. Say to them: "Put yourself in the painting and listen. Think of one of the sounds you would hear very clearly, but keep it in your head. Don't make the sound out loud until I tell you to do so. Is it clear in your imagination now? Good! When I raise my hands, I want you all to make your sounds at once, but WAIT! It's important to all stop together, too. When I lower my hands, stop making the sound. Let's try

6.3 Rousseau, Henri, *The Waterfall*, 1910, oil on canvas, 116.2 × 150.2 cm, The Helen Birch Bartlett Memorial Collection, 1926.262, The Art Institute of Chicago. All Rights Reserved, digital file ©The Art Institute of Chicago. All Rights Reserved

6.4 Avercamp, Hendrick, *Winter Landscape*, 1610–1620, oil on canvas, 13 × 24 in (33 × 61 cm), Courtesy of The St. Louis Art Museum. Photograph and digital image © 1996

it . . . 1 . . . 2 . . . 3 . . ."(Adults also enjoy this!) Now ask students to work together to write a circle (group) story. Begin with the sentence, "One day I was walking in . . ." Each person tells what their sound was, where they heard it, and adds one sentence to the story. You might need to rearrange sentences to help shape the story.

IMAGINARY ANIMALS

Some animals are real, some imaginary. Find paintings or decorative objects with creatures such as the sphinx, dragon, griffin, phoenix, centaur, and unicorn. Ask the students to identify which characteristics are real and which are imaginary. Then have them choose one animal to write a story about. A good art example for this activity would be *The Unicorn in Captivity* (figure 6.5), a beautiful tapestry from the Metropolitan Museum of Art. (The Metropolitan Museum of Art's Web page features a poem on the unicorn by Anne Morrow Lindbergh.)

WEATHER FORECAST

Another good sentence completion exercise that will expand observation skills involves using the five senses. Choose a painting with a lot of realis-

6.5 *The Unicorn in Captivity*, c. 1495–1505, silk, wool, silver and gilt threads, 145 × 99 in (368 × 251.5 cm), The Metropolitan Museum of Art, Gift of John D. Rockefeller Jr., 1937. (37.80.6) Photograph © 1988 The Metropolitan Museum of Art. All rights reserved, The Metropolitan Museum of Art

tic details and sensual clues, and ask students to give responses to the cues "I can see . . . , feel . . . , hear . . . " and so forth. Or choose paintings depicting several types of weather—snow scenes, rain, cloudy scenery— and ask them to try to create different weather forecasts. Choose a painting and have students write one paragraph about how the weatherman would describe this day and maybe what kind of day that would be for the child, describing how it looks, whether they like it, how it makes them feel, what they would wear, and what they would do for fun that day.

POSTCARD HOME

Use a painting of a place—a city street, a farm scene, or a boating scene—that is also available in a postcard reproduction. Ask students as a group to discuss the place they see in the painting. Use leading questions such as: "What is it like? Is it fun to be there? Why? What new things might they see in that place? What would be different from home? Why would they like to go there?" Then distribute postcards and ask students to write a message as if they were visiting that place and writing to their family at home. Mail the postcards.

COINS: ART IN YOUR POCKET

Many coins are miniature sculptures that contain a wealth of images, words, and symbols. This exercise doesn't require a museum visit or reproductions! Surprise students by telling them they probably have a sculpture in their pocket or at home. In the United States today, coins (as well as currency and stamps) are designed by artists who enter a competition, following guidelines put forth by the U.S. Mint. For example, U.S. coins today cannot depict a living person. The designs for the coin are drawn, then sculpted in clay, then molded in plaster, then cast in metal. Look at a penny with the students. Discuss the sculpture of Abraham Lincoln and why his image was a good choice to put on a much-used coin. The sculpture is not flat, but it is not fully round either, like the bust of a head would be. It is a type of sculpture known as relief, where the three-dimensional portion stands out against a flat background. Ask the students if they can find another element that is in very low relief (the Lincoln Memorial on the reverse side). Help the children to continue to explore this by asking: "Why is this a good type of sculpture for a coin? Why are different values of coins made in different sizes? Can you tell them apart in your pocket without looking?" Explain the motto and year on the coin. Compare several coins and examine the portraits, symbols, and mottoes on them. Explain what a motto is and ask students to write mottoes for their school, their class, and for themselves. (For more information on U.S. coins, check the Web page for the U.S. Mint or an encyclopedia.)

COINS

Coins, along with systems of weights and measures, evolved along with civilization. As people began to trade goods, they found metal to be a common value, and therefore useful for trading. At first, people traded with metal utensils. Then pieces of metal, the first "coins," were cut and stamped to mark their value or origin.

The form of coin we use today with a portrait of a political leader or heroic person began in ancient Greece. For example, the coin of the city-state Athens had a portrait head of the goddess Athena on one side, and an owl, the symbol of the goddess, on the obverse. Alexander the Great was the first historic person (i.e., rather than a divine personage) to be featured on a coin, underlying his connection to the Greek gods. This began a tradition of coinage we use today. Ancient coins were "struck"; pieces of hot metal were impressed between two molds to make the coin. Even in American colonial times the pine tree shilling, a coin made by the Sons of Liberty, was made this way. Modern coins, like the penny, are formed from a mold in much larger quantities.

NOTE

1. Gary Soulsman, "Framing a Language Arts Program," *The (Wilmington, Del.) News Journal,* 23 August 1994, D1–D4.

Words in Pictures

Art and writing merge in works of art that contain written language. The words and letters are symbols, recognizable icons that have greater weight than other signs, because their meaning is defined. Written language is a visual symbol system and as such has rich potential for artists.

SAMPLER

A sampler shows both the process and the proof of a young woman's education in historic time. For example, the sampler shown in figure 7.1 by Susanna Reed, age thirteen, offers a "sampling" of her abilities in a verse surrounded by a rich pattern of flowers and foliage, along with her name and date. It documents that she can read, write, draw, and do needlework, and depicts as well her discipline and proper upbringing. The verse reads:

> All you my Friends, who now expect to see
> A Piece of Working thus performed by me
> Cast but a Smile on this my mean Endeavor,
> I'll Strive to mend and be obedient ever.
> Tell me ye knowing and discerning few
> Where I may find a Friend both fine and true.
> Who dares stand by me when in deep Distress

And there his Love and Friendship most express.
Virtue's the chiefest Beauty of the Mind
The noblest Ornament of Human kind.
Virtue's our Safeguard and our guiding Star.
That stirs up Reason when our Senses err.

~SUSANNA REED / Her Work /
Aged 13 Years / 1827

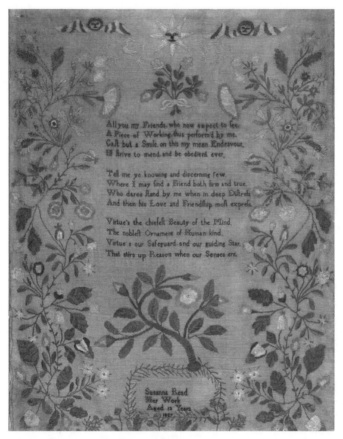

7.1 Reed, Susanna, *Sampler*, 1827, silk, linen, 28¾ × 23½ in (73.03 × 59.69 cm), Dallas Museum of Art, The Faith P. and Charles L. Bybee Collection, gift of Faith P. Bybee, 1991.B.316

What would the sampler of a young person today put forth? Would it be sewn or computer-generated? Ask students to create a rhyming verse in the form of the sampler (twelve lines of iambic pentameter) that presents their values. Create a "sampler" by framing the poem with drawings from nature.

TITLES

A title, whether for a poem, a book, or work of art, establishes a perspective on or theme for the work. Ask students to examine some titles, choosing at random from the bookshelves, for example: *How We Die, Journey to the Center, The Four Agreements, Obedience for Dog and Master, Murder Most Irish.* Ask students: "Does the title seem to be straightforward? Humorous? Expressive?"

Now consider titles for some works of art: *The Philosopher's Conquest, Seated Man; Untitled, Razor, Time and Tide.* Again ask students: "How are they like/unlike book titles? Why would an artist give a work a title? How does the artist create the titles?" Ask students to "title" several works of art. Then have them consider how each title influences the way we interpret the work. Ask students to choose one of the works of art and give it a title and then create an acrostic poem of the same title that interprets the work.

For this exercise, students worked in pairs. One paired retitled *Watch,* by Gerald Murphy, as *Takes a Licken and Keeps on Ticken* (figure 7.2). The interpretive acrostic follows:

*T*ic *T*oc
*A*rabesque
*K*eys
*E*venly
*S*lide

*A*bout

*L*ike
*I*ncrements
*C*ascading
*K*eenly
*E*ver
*N*ow

*A*rms
*N*eedling
*D*own

*K*icking
*E*ach other and
*E*very
*P*erson
*S*wiftly

7.2 Murphy, Gerald, *Watch*, 1925, oil on canvas, 78½ × 78⅞ in (199.39 × 200.36 cm), Dallas Museum of Art, Foundation for the Arts Collection, gift of the artist © 2001 Estate of Honoria Murphy Donnelly

*O*ut
*N*ear

*T*he
*I*mminent
*C*hoking
*K*nowing
*E*ternal
*N*ow

SIGNATURES

Many works of art contain words or written emblems within them. The most obvious example is the artist's signature, "Claude Monet" or "Winslow Homer." Some artists signed with a symbol; Whistler used a butterfly emblem. In the still life by Severin Roesen shown in

7.3 Roesen, Severin, *Fruit Still Life with Champagne Bottle*, 1848, oil on canvas, 24 × 30 in (60.96 × 76.2 cm), Dallas Museum of Art, gift of the Pauline Allen Gill Foundation, 2000.363.

figure 7.3, the artist created a *"trompe l'oeil"* (fool the eye) signature. He painted a corner of the tablecloth to look as though it was turned back to reveal the artist's initials in reversed embroidery. Then he signed his name next to it, making the illusion of embroidered initials seem more real.

Look at several examples of artists' signatures on paintings, sculptures, and pottery. Ask students to create their own "signature." Ask them: "Would they use a full name, initials, a symbol, or some combination? Printed or script? Clear or elusive? Why?"

INSCRIPTIONS: MOVING WORDS

Contemporary artist Jenny Holzer used LED electronic display signboards to create her artworks (figure 7.4). Words displayed in colored,

7.4 Holzer, Jenny, *I Am a Man*, 1987, electronic LED sign with green diodes, 112.5 × 10 × 4.5 in, Dallas Museum of Art, General Acquisitions Fund and matching grant from the National Endowment for the Arts 1988.57 © 2001 Jenny Holzer / Artists Rights Society (ARS), New York

moving "print" create a continuously changing, moving poem. This moment in figure 7.4, her work says "am a man . . . I protect . . . I am . . . I like a . . . bodies . . . I can . . . accident . . . ." Our sense of language causes us to automatically try to reconstruct meaning from

JENNY HOLZER'S *I AM A MAN*

The entirety of Holzer's piece shown in figure 7.4 is given here:

I am a man.
I enter space because
it empties me.
I chase people
around the house.
I sleep on my back
for sights of sex
that makes blood.
I protect what multiples
But I am not certain
that I love my body.
There is pleasure
in stopping my flesh
when it does wrong.
Getting what I want
makes me sick.
Why I fight is
not your business.
I like dying and I am sure
I can do it more than once.
I need perfection but
when I implement it

half of everyone dies.
I have a lot of accidents
and I think they are funny.
I employ people to make
my hours like dreams.
I like a circle of
bodies whose hands
do what they should.
I will kill you for
what you might do.

the fleeting words, but the meaning constantly changes. From protection to threat, assertion to denial, the words stream in an existential flow.

Ask students to create/invent a work of art with words where the meaning changes as words are moved. For example, strips of paper with words around a tube or an oatmeal box can be easily rearranged. Or stream words on the computer screen. Write words on a rolling pin or a ball. Create a rolling relief stamp of words from clay. See what the students can write and create!

CALLIGRAPHY

In the art traditions of the Western world, writing and painting are distinct activities. But in cultures like that of China and Japan, there is a long tradition of calligraphy, beautifully painted letters or words; writing is an art form just as painting is, and the two are related. Calligraphy completes a painting or creates a visual expression for a poem apart from any picture.

Japanese calligraphy is fluid and varies from heavy and dark to light and delicate. The form of the letters is expressive of mood, speed, and weight. Words and characters are painted with a brush. The tools of painting and calligraphy are the same. Ink is made from natural ground pigments mixed with resin to form an "inkstick." Ink is made when this stick is rubbed over a ridged stone block (inkstone) with water. The brush is made of animal hair and bamboo and constructed so that it retains a reservoir of ink within the bristles, allowing the ink to be released gradually. This permits great variety in brushstroke shade and strength.

The beautiful jade implements at this scholar's desk (figure 7.5) show the high esteem with which the painter/scholar (or literate) were held. Notice the bamboo brushes, the inkstick and inkstone, and the paper—these were the scholar's real "treasures." But the other objects are also treasures, such as the piece of jade curved to look like a piece of bamboo upon which the scholar rested his wrist while writing. There are also sculptures of scenes from nature, like a microcosm of the world. These sculptures or natural rocks whose formations cre-

7.5 Scholar's Desk, recreation using eighteenth-century objects, The Trammell and Margaret Crow Collection of Asian Art, Dallas, Texas, photo by Tom Jenkins

ated a similar effect were placed on the desk to help the scholar imagine creation.

NATURE SYMBOLISM

For a Japanese writer/scholar, poetry, painting, and writing were inseparable processes. The screen depicted in figure 7.6, *Bamboo and Calligraphy*, is a perfect example. It is decorated with panels, which contain alternating bands of paintings of bamboo, and calligraphy that tells a story about bamboo. According to the story, there were two young brothers who were born in a family and who became very different from each other as they grew older, yet they stayed firmly connected at the root. The story explains why bamboo is treasured. It has resilience; it can be bent to the ground, yet stays planted. This is a character trait to be emulated.

The screen was created by two artists who collaborated. The brushstrokes of the bamboo are very precise and controlled; the brushstrokes of the calligraphy are more free-flowing. Thus it sets up a conversation between the two styles of brushwork.

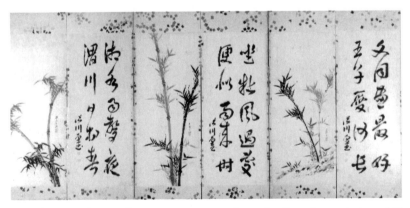

7.6 Keikai Gyokurin and Minagawa Kien, *Bamboo and Calligraphy*, c. 1800, six-fold screen; ink on paper bordered by gold-and silver-printed paper, Japan, The Trammell and Margaret Crow Collection of Asian Art, Dallas, Texas, Photo by Michael Bodycomb

The screen also contains several chops, red stamps with characters, which are inscriptions that are added after the work is done to indicate the date and school. Chops or signature seals were also used to identify the owners of the piece and can be used to trace its history.

Have students write a story about two brothers or sisters that embodies parallel traits of a natural element, such as water or a tree.

Sculpture: The Sense
of Form and Space

Writing about sculpture really requires the actual three-dimensional presence of the work (or a virtual facsimile). If you are looking at a photograph of a sculpture, you are missing essential elements, for a sculpture "owns" and interacts with the space it occupies and should be experienced in three dimensions.

That does not always require a museum visit, for there are many wonderful sculptures in our communities—memorials in banks, malls, and churches; sculptural duration of buildings; even cemeteries can provide a place to start. Here are some questions to use for a first writing exercise with sculpture.

- What is your first response to the work? What feeling does it evoke at first glance?
- When and where was it made? For what purpose? Where would it have been placed?
- What is the material, and why was it chosen?
- How are the surfaces handled? What is the resulting texture? What is the effect of color? Of light? Of the sculpture's surroundings?

- Is the sculpture more about a solid mass or constructed space?
- How does the artist convey movement?
- What are the main lines of force in the sculpture?
- What is the subject? Is it a realistic representation or an allegory? How does this sculpture differ from a painting of the same subject?
- If a figure, is it nude or clothed? Do the clothing and other drapery have a symbolic significance or affect the expression?
- What does the pose convey—stillness or movement?
- Is there an emotional expression implied in the pose (power, dignity, despair, conflict, repose)?
- Compare the figure to another sculpture: Is it more or less idealized than the other?

SCULPTURE

The unique characteristic of sculpture is the way it occupies space. Through the sculptural media—clay, wood, stone, or metal—the artist can render his or her idea into concrete form. In addition, its relationship to space and to light is dynamic and changeable. A sculpture can be experienced from many angles and in different lights and so becomes a successive series of perceptions. Light becomes an important aspect of the work, as well as the material from which a sculpture is made, as the receiver and reflector of that light.

The first sculptures of the Stone Age were probably suggested to the artist by the material, by the play of light on the projections of a cave wall that suggested a recognizable form. The artist enhanced the form to better represent his idea of the animal he hunted. By making a likeness of the animal from the mass of the stone, it is believed that he hoped to gain some power over the animal. To some extent, all sculptures contain an element of making an object, a simulacrum, which still, in primitive societies, is likely to be credited magical identification with its model.

The fact that these sculptures remain demonstrates another important aspect of sculpture—its endurance. This quality led artists to choose sculpture as the art form to represent ideas of lasting significance and memories. A sculpture is a work of art with a sense of history.

The various forms sculpture can take—nude, figure, animal, monster, mask, decoration—continue throughout history. The figure was a dominant theme in sculpture because of man's anthropomorphic conceptions of deity, but ultimately because of the capacity for beauty and expressiveness in the human body. It was also a challenging structure with its tension between muscle, bone, and flesh, and therefore a demonstration of technical competence.

Sculptural Processes

The basic methods of producing sculpture changed very little from ancient times until the advent of new modern conceptions of what constituted sculpture.

Carving

To carve a figure from a block of stone, the artist must have in mind a clear idea of the form he or she wants to emerge and an understanding of the effects of carving on the material. Usually a model is shaped from clay or wax. Then the main lines of the sculpture are marked on the block (called pointing) by a specialized artisan, who does the rough first cutting. The artist then finishes the sculpture with a chisel. Refinements of the surface can be achieved by using fine rasps, and a highly polished surface can be achieved by rubbing with pumice or sand. Often a patina of oil or wax is added to enhance the finish.

Wood is carved in a similar way. Occasionally the wood is hollowed out to reduce the effects of humidity. The surface is then marked with chalk and carved with a chisel. Finishing might include the addition of paint, gold, or oils.

(continued)

SCULPTURE (cont.)

Modeling

Modeling is the building up of a form by hand from clay. It gives the artist an advantage over carving, in terms of being able to change the form more often, and it also gives the work a freshness and immediacy that is possible in carving only for the most skilled artist. Permanent clay figures are made of terra-cotta and fired. Smaller statuettes are built of solid clay, but larger pieces require a wooden or wire armature that allows an even thickness of clay to be fired; the armature is removed, and the piece is fired hollow. The sculpture can be finished with a variety of glazes that are fired on to produce a glassy finish. Modeling is also a preparatory step to carving and casting. Additives such as wax or oil are sometimes added to the clay to prevent its hardening or cracking.

Casting

The process of casting was used during ancient times, and although neglected during the Middle Ages, it was revived during the Renaissance. There are two main types of casting—sand process and lost wax. In sand process casting, damp sand is tightly compressed against a plaster pattern, between iron flashing. The plaster is removed and the sand dried, then liquid bronze is poured into the sand-lined flashing mold. When the mold has cooled, it is opened and the sand is removed from the cast bronze. The lost wax (*cire perdue*) method involves several stages. First, a negative is made of the model to be cast. A heavy coating of wax is brushed inside the negative mold to make a hollow wax duplicate of the model. After adding gates and vents to allow for pouring the metal, the wax model is coated inside and out with a heat-resistant compound that makes a new mold. When this is heated, the wax will melt and run out, and liquid bronze can be poured into the mold. The figure is then cleaned with acid and finished.

Patina refers to the finish of a bronze. A natural patina is the result of chemical processes that leave an incrustation on the surface of the bronze, usually of a greenish color. Sometimes artificial patinas are applied to achieve a desired finish or to protect the bronze.

Construction

Construction emerged as a sculptural method with the advent of modern art and the use of collage and assemblage. Objects or parts of objects are sometimes assembled in a new and thought-provoking way. Construction sculptures deal with the problems of space and often have moving parts, as in the mobile. In construction, the artist builds the sculpture from wire, wood, metal, plastic, and other found materials. In this method, the creative working process of the artist is more apparent, and the nature of the material he or she chooses has much to do with the final effect.

FIGURAL SCULPTURE—PYGMALION

Three-dimensional art forms, such as sculpture and architecture, contain or occupy space, and we experience these physically. Each person occupies not only his or her own body, but a certain amount of space around it. We say someone is "invading our space." Art forms also have a presence in space.

The human figure has been a dominant theme in sculpture since ancient times, when most sculptures represented divinities. Ultimately the beauty, structural complexity, and expressiveness of the human form have immense appeal. Perhaps because of this physicality, we also tend to project human qualities onto forms such as automobiles, houses, and chairs!

Because realistic figural sculpture literally "stands in" for the objects, it is considered a simulacrum. Ask students to choose a figural sculpture and write about the sculpture "coming to life," either in the time it was created or in the present. They should develop a character for the sculpture and describe the person's appearance, stance, gestures, energy level, movement, and how he or she interacts with others.

ABSTRACT SCULPTURE AS A FIGURE

Traditionally, the most important subject for sculpture was the human figure. In the twentieth century, artists often reduced the figure to an abstract or abbreviated form. Still, these works often express the energy, the sense of movement, and the tension of the figure.

Writing about abstract sculpture as a figure helps students to decode the formal language. Use the following ideas to help students develop these skills:

1. Write about an abstract sculpture as a figure.
2. Consider the lines of force, bearing, weight and mass, and movement or stillness.
3. Describe the energy and gestures of the person you imagine.

DAVID SMITH—*CUBI XVII*

David Smith was born in Indiana in 1906. His parents instilled in him a sense of hard work, which was matched by his boundless physical energy. Smith found his calling as a sculptor while working with welded iron and steel in a Studebaker plant in South Bend in 1932. He worked in New York, creating sculptures of wood, metal, and iron while maintaining his ideological commitment to the "working men" he had known in Indiana.

During the 1940s, he continued to work as a welder, as well as to create sculptures, teach, and write. Working on locomotives and tanks needed for the war effort, he developed a new sense of scale. After the war, Smith built a studio away from the New York art circles and created abstract metal sculptures based on the figure. His *Cubi* series, of which figure 8.1 is an example, of the 1960s, made of stainless steel cylinders and tube, represent the culmination of his style.

8.1 Smith, David, *Cubi XVII*, 1963, polished stainless steel, 107¾ × 64⅜ × 38⅛ in
(273.68 × 163.53 × 96.85 cm), Dallas Museum of Art, The Eugene and Margaret
McDermott Art Fund, Inc. 1965.32.MCD © Estate of David Smith / Licensed by
VAGA, New York, NY

ALL THE ANGLES

The distinguishing feature of sculpture is that it exists in space. You can't
really "see" a sculpture in the round from a single angle or photograph.
The different shapes that emerge as the sculpture is viewed from different angles (as well as different qualities of light and atmosphere) give it
an ever-changing expression.

Henry Moore said that a sculptor wants to know what a thing is like
from every angle possible. Instruct students to walk around a work of art,

look at the work from above and below, and write all the different perspectives they see. Have them focus on a vivid description. Ask: "What associations do you have with each shifting perspective?" Take a line from each different viewpoint and collage them together into a poem. If this is a group project, have each member choose a favorite line and read it, then collage these lines together (activity by Shin Yu Pi).

A group of six writing on Barbara Hepworth's sculpture *Contrapuntal Form* (figure 8.2) came up with the following. (Number indicates order in the group—the contribution of the last member to share results fit best at the beginning of the poem.)

5   Light pierces the wedge of ice
1   Shallow yet deep
2   I see two eyes, yet I wonder if they can see me
3   The penetrations in the smooth flat surface
     Harbor the forms of reflected light
4   Two holes always let the potential leak out.

~KATIE BERLIN, VICKI SHAPIRO, BOB MANAHAN,
ADRON GIBBONS, KATHY WALSH-PIPER

A TACTILE PLACE

Part of our sense of place is made up of the materials in it. Artists who are true to the natural materials they work with bring a sense of place to the art. For example, the English landscape and nature heavily influenced Henry Moore—he identified very strongly with the physical world around him, using forms and shapes from nature in his work. The qualities of stone or wood both determine and inhabit the sculptures made from these materials.

Have students think of a physical place in their own life that has been important and formative in their development. Have them focus on an image from this place that embodies their feelings about this place. (For Henry Moore, this might have been sea pebbles, rocks, or cliffs.) Tell students to describe in physical detail this image/object and what it symbolizes for them. What meaning is reflected or revealed through its physical form or matter? An example of this activity is given here:

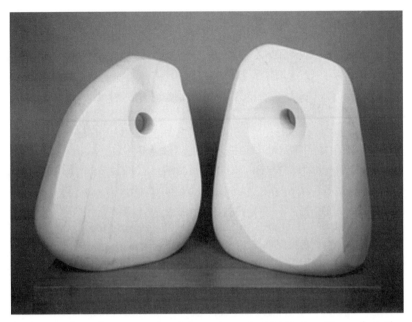

8.2 Hepworth, Barbara, *Contrapuntal Form (Mycenae)*, 1965, Barbara Hepworth © Alan Bowness, Hepworth Estate; Dallas Museum of Art, gift of Mr. and Mrs. James H. Clark

The beach at Santa Monica is hazy and cluttered. With the highway there, it's easy to be distracted from nature. But the water eventually pulls you in. First mesmerized by stones and glass, my eyes are fixed at the shore along the beach. I pull my eyes away, resting them on the surf, and it rolls backward, sucking water through the stones and sand and creating a tinkling, rumbling, jingle of the small stones that is delightful. I sit in the sand and wait for that sound to come again, sifting water and rock, past and present, sighing back into the ocean, back and forth.

USING CHANCE FOR INSPIRATION— DADA AND SURREALISM

The horror of World War I caused a reaction in intellectual circles in Europe, a questioning of traditional values and premises that were based on the concepts of reason and order. The sense that reason and order had not prevented the disastrous war led a group of writers and artists to turn to the nonrational, the intuitive, and the element of chance. Among them, Jean Arp was both a poet and a sculptor who used the element of "chance" to shape his art. Arp let pieces of paper or string fall to the floor and based poems or collages on the results. As the object took shape, forms emerged that suggested organic shapes and figures. Arp called any interior circle that emerged a "navel," in keeping with the essentially figurative nature of sculpture. He would name the sculpture after it had been created, sometimes adding another layer of meaning.

Allow students to try the "chance" method. To warm up, let each student drop two or three pieces of string on the floor and explain what type of figure he or she sees. Then use words cut from magazines or newspapers, pulled at random from an envelope, to assemble a word poem or to use as the basis for describing one of Arp's sculptures. Here are the results of using words to describe Arp's *Sculpture Classique* (figure 8.3) in a gallery workshop. (Words used from the cutouts are in parentheses.)

8.3 Arp, Jean, *Sculpture Classique*, 1960, bronze, 50 × 8¾ × 8 in (127 × 22.23 × 20.32 cm), Dallas Museum of Art, Foundation for the Arts Collection, given in memory of Mary Seeger O'Boyle by her family and friends, 1966.13. FA © 2001 Artists Rights Society (ARS), New York / VG Bild-Kunst, Bonn

Words (wealth, objects, figure, mystery, typical, key, power, looking)
Wealth is only objects,
But this figure is mystery.
No one's figure is typical
You find the key to your power by looking at yourself.

~KATIE BERLIN

SENSE OF PLACE: MUGHAL FACADE

Sculpture is often a part of architectural exteriors. Architectural forms can transform our sense of a space. Elaborate floral and geometrical forms were carved in stone to create this Mughal facade (figure 8.4) from the second story of a palace in India. The Mughals came to India from the West, bringing their Islamic culture. The practice of Islam forbade

8.4 *Mughal Façade*, North India, Mughal period (1526–1756), 18th century, red sandstone carved in jali and half-jali techniques, The Trammell and Margaret Crow Collection of Asian Art, Dallas, Texas, Photo by Tom Jenkins

artists to use human forms; their decoration often included designs from nature or geometric designs. The tracery of patterns and graceful arches create an elegant facade for the building, but it also was functional. The stones below are carved in relief; the stones in the gallery above are carved all the way through, creating a screen so someone standing behind it could see out but could not be seen very well from the outside. This treatment, called Jali, was created for the Muslim women who were not permitted to venture into the public space.

Over the central doorway there is a graceful arch. The shape is often used in Mughal architecture, but here it also functions to divert rainwater from the roof. Have students describe the sense of space created by this building and write about this building as a personality. Would it be male or female? Secretive or open? Friendly or forbidding? Reserved or outgoing?

Nine

Museum Visit Journal

O ne visit to an art museum is like a day in a city park; it may be completely different the next time! Not only do exhibitions change, but also your mood and interests change. So even if you and your students have been to the museum before, go again ready to absorb and reflect, to discover something new in the museum—or in yourself. Ask students: "What do you remember from your first visit? What was your favorite visit?" One of the most moving presentations I've ever heard was at an art teachers' conference in South Carolina. One of the speakers, a teacher, recounted her memories of several museum visits in a moving series of reminiscences.

On another visit, consider the sense of the place. Use these questions to start a discussion: "What does the building and entryway say about the kind of place it is? Where is the site—on a busy street or high on a hill? What is the feeling and mood—is it a sanctuary, an old-fashioned trea- sure trove, or a modern palace of art? What is the identity of your favorite museum?" Have students consider the museum as a beloved teacher or friend and write about it as a person—a muse!

For this visit, don't try to see everything. Choose an area to explore, and have your students try some basic writing approaches like these:

List: Make a list of ways to think about and what to look for in a work of art—as many as you can.

Describe: Write a description of one work that is so detailed that a person who had never seen the artwork could draw it from your description. Choose very specific adjectives for each item in your description.

Interpret: Remember that interpretation says what you think the work is really about, what it means and expresses, how the use of media contributes to that effect, and why you think it was made. Your opinion is your own, but it should be based on describable facts of the work. Be persuasive! Refer to what you see in the work to defend your interpretation.

Stream of consciousness: Write about the experience of standing in the museum looking at a work of art. Include unrelated thoughts, feelings, sounds, frustrations, puzzles or questions, and delights. This is not about the art work per se, but about your experience.

Conversation: Create a conversation between two works of art: two portraits, a portrait and an object, an object and a landscape, and so forth.

Ask the students what they notice about the process of looking and writing. They may just want to wander, letting art catch their eye, but they should notice what they see and feel. They may find themselves thinking about the time and place the works were made, the artist at work, or their own personal ideas and relationships. They may stop and stare at a work for the sheer wonder of it. This is the best kind of visit.

Have students write a label. Say: "Just for yourself, try to rewrite (or supply!) a label for one work in a gallery. Be free with your advice. The label should show visitors what to look for and pay attention to." Here are some examples:

"*Look out!* There's some serious stuff in here."
"*Pay attention to details here.* These prints look alike at first, but the genius is in the lines."
"You can still smell the paint in this gallery!"
"Why do we have museums?"

Have students think about the act of saving precious objects from the past. Students can relate in that they might collect things from their own life as mementos. The museum is a culture's collection of things that are deemed important. Have students think about why the museum exists. Say: "Museums are a fairly recent phenomenon; most big urban museums in our country were created in the late 1900s. Why does the museum we are visiting exist? Watch the visitors; why do you think they come? What is meaningful about their visit? Could the museum be replaced by a Web site?" Then have students write an essay defending or rejecting the need for the museum.

ROLE PLAYING: OWNING AN OBJECT

Some of the most interesting objects in the museum are not paintings or sculptures, but objects once used in rituals and in everyday life. Find a gallery of decorative arts. Have students choose one object and imagine a character unlike themselves who would choose it. The following is an example from a student who viewed the portrait *Champagne Glass* (figure 9.1):

> My, My if only my Mama could see me now! This is the most exciting place on earth. Everyone looks so nice—look at 'em dancin' and drinkin' and . . . oh my, look at that tray! Oh, I wonder which is mine?

9.1 Dougherty, George, *Champagne Glass*, 1928, glass, blown, molded, $6\frac{1}{2} \times 4\frac{1}{4}$ in, Dallas Museum of Art, 20th-Century Design Fund, 1996.23

The champagne—Oh I love champagne. Oh, they're never gonna believe me when I tell 'em I was here! Look at that glass—it's my drink element how'd they make that little square in the stem like that? Its so, . . . so *modern!* When I'm finished, I'll stick my finger through that square and twirl the glass around while I dance. ~PAMELA RODY

NOSTALGIA

Students could also choose a decorative object and use it as a springboard for nostalgic writing. One student's example is given here:

Mom always get herself in a sweat over Thanksgiving Dinner. Red faced, pushing the hair off her forehead with the back of her hand. She never wanted much help—sometimes she'd let me mash the potatoes with that smasher thing. But her dinner always turned out great. She'd set the table with the "good stuff"—Czechoslovakian crystal goblets, Wedgewood plates, and she'd bring out the cabbage serving dishes— that's what my siblings and I called them. I was always intrigued by those serving dishes—molded porcelain or whatever it was—green and lumpy and veined like big cabbage leafs. Gorgeous table—every year we'd take a picture of it. The table—all set up pretty—the turkey and dressing and stuffing and mashed potatoes and gravy. And we'd always exchange glances and raised eyebrows. And that one weird quirk of Mom's—the oyster casserole that no one ate but . . . ~PAMELA RODY

SENSE OF SPACE

Most museums try to create a special, rarefied environment where art is "set apart" for contemplation. There is usually the bustle of coat check, tickets, information, and maps at the entrance—maybe a shop or café also. But even the busiest museum usually has a quiet corner, an oasis where people can write and respond and try to define the setting they are in. Have students see if they can find a "set apart" place and write about the museum as a place to look and think.

TIME TRIP

Another fascinating aspect of museums is the sense of time. Many of the objects on display actually existed and were created in a different time.

Other aspects are the time it took to create the work, the sense of the artist's hand, the time it takes to look at the work. Tell students to find a work that gives them a feeling for and helps them to imagine another time. See if they can put themselves back in that time and write about a day in the life of the object when it was new.

EAVESDROPPING

It's not really polite to eavesdrop, but if you spend time in a busy gallery or exhibition you are bound to overhear some interesting comments on works of art, as well as other subjects. Have students take notes of snippets of conversation or reactions they overhear while visiting a gallery or museum and assemble an imaginary conversation about a work of art from their "collection."

SELF-PORTRAIT

Have students find a self-portrait while visiting an art gallery. Ask: "Did the artist conceal or reveal the use of mirror? What setting or props did the artist choose, and why? Does the portrait seem realistic?" Now have the students turn the "mirror" on themselves (of course, the image in the mirror is reversed, so they may want to try two mirrors, or a photograph, to see themselves the way others see them). Have them write a descriptive and expressive self-portrait of themselves.

THE PICTURE I WANT TO PAINT

Even if you can't draw or paint, you can imagine a work of art you'd like to create yourself. Every work of art starts with a concept; in fact, to some artists, the concept itself is the work of art. A work of art needs two elements: a visual image rendered in a media with expressive skill. Have students focus on those elements and write their conception of a work of art. Here's a portion of a description of a work that Paul Gauguin planned to create but never did.

> It is six meters long and two meters high. Why those dimensions? Because that is the entire width of my studio, and because working up high tires me exceedingly. The canvas is already stretched, prepared, carefully smoothed, not a knot, not a crease, not a spot. Just think, it is going to be a masterpiece.

In terms of geometrical composition, the lines will start from the middle, elliptical at first, then undulating, until you come to the ends. The main figure will be woman turning into a statue, still remaining alive yet becoming an idol. The figure will stand out against a clump of trees such as do not grow on earth but only in Paradise. You see what I mean, don't you! This is not Pygmalion's statue coming alive and becoming human, but woman becoming idol. Nor is this Lot's wife being turned into a pillar of salt: great God, no!

Fragrant flowers are seen on all sides, children frolic in this garden, girls pick fruit heaped up in enormous baskets; robust young men in graceful poses lay them at the idol's feet. The over-all mood of the painting should be grave, like a religious incantation, melancholy and at the same time gay like the children. Ah! I almost forgot: I also want to put in some adorable little black pigs, their snout snuffling at the good food that will be eaten, their desire shown by the way there tails tremble with eagerness.

My figures will be life-size in the foreground, but here's the hitch: the rules of perspective are going to force me to place the horizon very high up and my canvas is only two meters high, which means I will not be able fully to include the superb mango trees in my garden.

How difficult painting is! I will trample on the rules and I will be stoned to death. To set the mood of gravity, the colors will be grave. To set the mood of gaiety, the colors will be light, melodious as sheaves of wheat. How shall I manage, a painting that is dark and light at the same time? Of course, there is the "in-between-the-two" solution that generally satisfies people but which I do not like at all. My God, how difficult painting is when you want to express your thoughts with pictorial rather that literary means. The painting I want to do is certainly far from being done, the desire is greater than my power, my weakness is enormous and weakness, hmm!. Let us sleep. [1]

NOTE

1. See Daniel Guerin, ed., *The Writings of a Savage: Paul Gauguin*, trans. Eleanor Levieux (New York: Viking, 1986).

An Educator's Response

What a delight to see this book come to fruition. In the summer of 1990 I took a course in impressionism and post-impressionism at the National Gallery of Art in Washington, D.C. Kathy Walsh-Piper was one of the instructors for the course, and beyond the expected elements of the classes was the opportunity to sit in one of the galleries and select a painting for a writing assignment.

My focus dramatically changed then from learning details and facts about paintings to trying to see the subjects through the artist's eyes, striving to translate into words the visual images that until then had rested on the surface of the canvas. Perhaps true art students do that naturally, can feel the emotions of the creator, can synthesize with the intent, not merely be awed by the result. But for an ordinary person, this was a breakthrough.

What does one do with such a discovery? Share it with others. And as a teacher, I took the lessons with me back to my classroom and began sharing them with my students. I already used music and film to expand their abilities to read and write and think; now I tried paintings as well.

The following examples derive from those classes. What I must add is a note about the high interest level and willingness to take risks that these classes produced. Whether with ninth graders or twelfth graders, every such effort was met with enthusiasm and fine explorations by the students. In the summer sessions, I became an imitator: I took the writing to the National Gallery of Art and let my students relive my own experience.

The old saying that a picture is worth a thousand words emphasizes the unspoken (and indescribable) depth of many paintings. It is a revealing three-step exercise to ask someone to draw a scene, then describe it in words. The originator then hands the written description to another person who is asked to draw the scene described by the words on the page. The difficulty of expressing a visual, sensual scene in words is immediately evident. Perhaps even a thousand words would not have been enough to accomplish the task successfully.

However, there is another way to read "a picture is worth a thousand words," and that is by emphasizing the little word "is." A picture *is* worth a thousand words. That shifts the focus from a literal attempt to duplicate the picture in words to a more creative sense of revealing the picture's impression. It acknowledges that this picture does possess a depth that is truly worth the effort to try to express its qualities in writing. The hitch is that the writing cannot be vague, abstract, or too figurative itself, or it will not accurately convey the picture.

How does one capture the essence of a painting, for example, without reducing it to a list of what is in the painting and without being so abstruse that it actually makes the painting less meaningful? This may well require a blend of the Western technique of analysis and the Eastern technique of synthesis.

For instance, consider *Horse and Train* by Canadian artist Alex Colville (figure E.1). This night scene looks almost realistic, but it cannot be. A powerful dark horse (center-right foreground), ears back, is galloping down the railroad tracks directly at an oncoming steam locomotive (left distance, curving out of the horizon of the prairie). One bright circle of light, the train's single headlight, breaks the darkened scene.

Here again, the list of what is in the painting is brief and clear: horse, train, tracks, light, darkness, flat land, horizon. What is not shown? Even a short time with the painting leads to the realization that there is more, something powerful and intense and frightening in this animal's headlong and intentional rushing at the steel engine of the train. It is time for the thousand words:

The still prairie is innocent of the looming disaster. The moonless cloud-dappled sky eases to the flat and dark horizon unknown miles in the distance, and gentle plains grasses wait quietly for the crisping warmth of tomorrow's sun. It is a setting for pioneers, for adventurers trekking west. And surely somewhere near—within a hundred miles, say—a campfire fends off the night fears as Westering people pause on their way to a bountiful future.

But here the silence is terrifying. There should be roars and guttural challenges, but no noise deafens the reality of the clash nor lessens its terror. Two shining lines of track, glistening steely in the onrushing moonlamp of the locomotive, bend past where we stand, and from somewhere beyond the horizon an endless train thunders from the infinite darkness directly toward us. Its monstrous, implacable power will slide by slightly to our right and leave us witnesses, mourners.

For what passes will not be a train only; also an age; also a love, a symbol. And we will be left with more than a sense of heat and

E.1 Colville, Alex. *Horse and Train*, 1954, glazed tempera on masonite. Courtesy of Alex Colville; Art Gallery of Hamilton, gift of Dominion Foundries and Steel, Ltd. 1957

sound and rushing wind and a magnetic pull toward the piston-churning destruction that has passed. We will stand awe-struck for generations, a hollowness pounding in our throats at the loss we have been powerless to prevent.

Also on the tracks is a horse, a powerful black stallion whose bunched muscles pound the man-made tracks in a defiant charge against the train. Its ears are flattened back, its high, rear haunches drive its natural power, its eyes are trapped in the moonlamp's gravity. It is the grace and poise and swiftness of all things natural, the beautiful perfection of the un-manmade, and being so, it is doomed against the train.

And we must stand silent at the passing.

In searching for this sense of understanding, the writer will explore implications beyond the literal facts of the painting and begin to synthesize with the painting and, if lucky, the artist. One result, beyond greater appreciation, is that the writer, having now become part of the creative process, is unlikely ever to forget this painting.

Of course each person's words express the person as well as the painting, which may be the point. Writing about paintings is a creative act: It lifts out of us ideas we may not have known were there, phrases we have never before used, understandings we had not linked before this moment.

Students often seem astonished by the fact that if they do not write these words down, they will never be written. Only that one person could have written the piece about *Horse and Train*: All others would be different. Equally valid, equally new, different. They are personal; they are informative; they are learning. This is discovery.

Each painting *is* worth a thousand words.

~ED SUNDT

Bibliography

Albertine, Sarah, and Danielle Pastor. Project for "Introduction to Medieval History." Fordham University, spring 1997.

Allen, T. D. *Writing to Create Ourselves: New Approaches for Teachers, Students, and Writers*. Norman: University of Oklahoma, 1982.

Arneson, H. H. *History of Modern Art*. 2d ed. New York: Prentice-Hall, 1975.

Arnheim, Rudolf. *The Power of the Center*. Berkeley: University of California Press, 1998.

Art Institute of Chicago. *Masterworks in the Art Institute of Chicago*. Selected by James N. Wood and Katherine C. Lee. Chicago: Art Institute of Chicago, 1998.

Audubon, John James. *Audubon, by Himself*. Edited by Alice Ford. Garden City, N.Y.: National History Press, 1969.

Barnet, Sylvan. *A Short Guide to Writing about Art*. Boston: Little, Brown, 1981.

Bate, W. Jackson, and David Perkins, eds. *British & American Poets: Chaucer to the Present*. San Diego, Calif.: Harcourt Brace Jovanovich, 1986.

Bermingham, Peter. *The Art of Poetry*. Vols. I–IV. Washington, D.C.: Smithsonian Institution, 1976.

Bishop, Wendy. *Released into Language: Options for Teaching Creative Writing*. Urbana, Ill.: National Council of Teachers of English, 1990.

Bolker, Joan, ed. *The Writer's Home Companion: An Anthology of the World's Best Writing Advice, from Keats to Kuniz*. New York: Henry Holt, 1997.

Brande, Dorothea. *Becoming a Writer*. New York: Jeremy P. Tarcher/Putnam, 1934.

Brockbank, Philip. *The Creativity of Perception: Essays in the Genesis of Literature and Art*. Oxford: Basil Blackwell, 1991.

Bunchman, Janis, and Stephanie Bissell Briggs. *Activities for Creating: Pictures and Poetry*. Worcester, Mass.: Davis Publication, 1994.

Burn, Barbara, ed. *Masterpieces of the Metropolitan Museum of Art*. New York: Metropolitan Museum of Art, 1993.

Carmean, E. A., Jr. *David Smith*. Washington, D.C.: National Gallery of Art, 1982.

Colley, Ann C. *The Search for Synthesis in Literature and Art*. Athens: University of Georgia Press, 1990.

Collom, Jack, and Sheryl Noethe. *Poetry Everywhere*. New York: Teachers and Writers Collaborative, 1994.

Dallas Museum of Art. *Dallas Museum of Art: A Guide to the Collection*. Dallas: Dallas Museum of Art, 1997.

Daniel, Howard. *Devils, Monsters, and Nightmares*. New York: Abelard-Schuman, 1964.

Department of Museum Education, Art Institute of Chicago. *Looking to Write/Writing to See: A Course in Visual and Language Arts*. Chicago: Art Institute of Chicago, 1996.

Dietrich, Linnea, and Diane Smith-Hurd. "Feminist Approaches to the Survey." *Art Journal* 54 (fall 1995): 44–47.

Edgar, Christopher, and Ron Padgett, eds. *Educating the Imagination: Essays and Ideas for Teachers and Writers*. New York: Teachers and Writers Collaborative, 1994.

Edwards, Iowerth Eiddon Stephen. *Treasures of Tutankhamun*. New York: Metropolitan Museum of Art, 1976.

Engle, Paul. *On Creative Writing*. New York: E. P. Dutton, 1963.

European Portraits 1600–1900 in the Art Institute of Chicago. Chicago: Art Institute of Chicago, 1986.

Ferlinghetti, Lawrence. *When I Look at Pictures*. Salt Lake City, Utah: Gibbs Smith, 1990.

Finn, David. *How to Look at Sculpture*. New York: Harry N. Abrams, 1989.

———. *How to Visit a Museum*. New York: Harry N. Abrams, 1985.

Franck, Frederick. *Art as a Way: A Return to the Spiritual Roots*. New York: Crossroad, 1981.

Gaugh, Harry F. *The Vital Gesture: Franz Kline*. New York: Abbeville Press, 1985.

Gealt, Adelheid M. *Looking at Art: A Visitor's Guide to Museum Collections*. New York: R. R. Bowker, 1983.

Gilbert, Rita. *Living with Art*. Boston: McGraw-Hill, 1998.

Goldberg, Natalie. *Writing Down the Bones: Freeing the Writer Within*. Boston: Shambhala, 1986.

Goode, Erica. "When People See a Sound and Hear a Color." *New York Times on the Web*. www.nytimes.com, 1999 [accessed 30 March 2001].

Gordon, Robert, and Andrew Forge. *Monet*. New York: Harry N. Abrams, 1983.

Graham-Dixon, Andrew. *Paper Museum: Writings about Painting, Mostly*. New York: Viking, 1997.

Greenthal, Kathryn. *Augustus Saint-Gaudens: Master Sculptor*. New York: Metropolitan Museum of Art, 1985.

Guerin, Daniel, ed. *The Writings of a Savage: Paul Gauguin*. Translated by Eleanor Levieux. New York: Viking, 1986.

Hamilton, Dorothy G. *Picture Thoughts: Critical Thinking through Visual Arts*. Columbia, Md.: Hamilton Associates, 1989.

Harris, Neil. *Cultural Excursions: Marketing Appetites and Cultural Tastes in Modern America*. Chicago: University of Chicago Press, 1990.

Harvey, Eleanor Jones. *The Painted Sketch: American Impressions from Nature 1830–1880*. Dallas: Dallas Museum of Art, 1998.

Hausman, Carl R. *Metaphor and Art: Interactionism and Reference in the Verbal and Nonverbal Arts*. Cambridge: Cambridge University Press, 1998.

Haverstock, Mary Sayre. *Indian Gallery: The Story of George Catlin*. New York: Four Winds Press, 1973.

Hirsch, Edward, ed. *Transforming Vision: Writers on Art*. Chicago: Little, Brown, 1994.

Hollander, John. *Ryhme's Reason: A Guide to English Verse*. New Haven, Conn.: Yale University Press, 1981.

Janson, H. W., ed. *The Nature of Representation: A Phenomenological Inquiry*. New York: New York University Press, 1961.

Johns, Jasper. *Jasper Johns: Writings, Sketchbook Notes, Interviews*. Edited by Kirk Varnedoe. New York: Museum of Modern Art, 1996.

Joselow, Beth Baruch. *Writing without the Muse: 50 Beginning Exercises for the Creative Writer*. Brownsville, Oreg.: Story Line Press, 1995.

Kale, Shelly, and Lisa Vihos. *My Museum Journal: A Writing and Sketching Book*. Los Angeles: J. Paul Getty Museum, 2000.

Kandinsky, Wassily. *On the Spiritual in Art*. New York: Solomon R. Guggenheim Foundation, for the Museum of Non-Objective Painting, 1946.

Karcheski, Walter J. *Arms and Armor in the Art Institute of Chicago*. Chicago: Art Institute of Chicago, 1995.

Kellan, Ann. "Ever Taste a Shape, or Smell a Color?: Neurologist Explores Strange World of Synesthesia," www.cnn.com,1995 [accessed 30 March 2001].

Kemper, Dave, Ruth Nathan, and Patrick Sebranek. *Writers Express: A Handbook for Young Writers, Thinkers and Learners*. Wilmington, Mass.: Write Source, 1995.

Kepes, Gyorgy, ed. *Sign, Image, Symbol*. London: Studio Vista, 1966.

Kitson, Norma. *Creative Writing: A Handbook with Exercises and Examples*. Harare: Baobab Books, 1997.

Knapp, Bettina L. *Word, Image, Psyche*. Tuscaloosa: University of Alabama Press, 1985.

Knobler, Nathan. *The Visual Dialogue: An Introduction to the Appreciation of Art*. New York: Holt, Rinehart and Winston, 1967.

Koch, Kenneth. *Wishes, Lies, and Dreams: Teaching Children to Write Poetry*. New York: Harper and Row, 1970.

Kristeva, Julia. *Desire in Language: Semiotic Approach to Literature and Art*. Edited by Leon S. Roudiez, translated by Alice Thomas Hardine Gora and Leon S. Roudiez. New York: Columbia University Press, 1980.

Levine, Sherrie. *Constantin Brancusi 1876–1957*. Philadelphia: Philadelphia Museum of Art, 1995.

Lippincott, Louise. *Edvard Munch: Starry Night*. Los Angeles: J. Paul Getty Museum, 1988.

Lowderbaugh, Thomas E. *Making Sense: Writing from Objects, a Smithsonian Approach*. Washington, D.C.: Office of Elementary and Secondary Education: Smithsonian Institution.

Maisel, Eric. *Fearless Creating: A Step-By-Step Guide to Starting and Completing Your Work of Art*. New York: Jeremy P. Tarcher/Putman, 1995.

Masterpieces of the J. Paul Getty Museum: Paintings. Los Angeles: Thame and Hudson and the J. Paul Getty Museum, 1997.

McCoy, Garnett, ed. *David Smith*. New York: Praeger Publishers, 1973.

McShine, Kynaston, ed. *Joseph Cornell*. New York: Museum of Modern Art, New York, 1980.

Mealy, Virginia T. *From Reader to Writer: Creative Writing in the Middle Grades Using Picture Books*. Metuchen, N.J.: Scarecrow, 1986.

Mierse, William E., with Jean Kiedaisch and Sue Dinitz. "Fitting Writing into the Survey." *Art Journal* 54 (fall 1995): 82.

Mueller, Lavonne, and Jerry D. Reynolds. *Creative Writing: Forms and Techniques*. Lincolnwood, Ill.: NTC Publishing Group, 1990.

Murphy, Richard. *Imaginary Words: Notes on a New Curriculum*. New York: Teachers and Writers, 1974.

Museum Staff. *J. Paul Getty Museum: Handbook of the Collection*. Malibu, Calif.: J. Paul Getty Museum, 1986.

Myers, Jack Fredrick. *The Language of Visual Art: Perception as a Basis for Design*. Fort Worth, Tex.: Holt, Rinehart, and Winston, 1989.

Nights and Lights: 19th and 20th Century American Nocturne Paintings. Cincinnati: Taft Museum, 1985.

Olson, Carol Booth, ed. *Practical Ideas for Teaching Writing as a Process*. Sacramento, Calif.: California Department of Education, 1987.

Padgett, Ron, ed. *The Teachers and Writers Handbook of Poetic Forms*. New York: Teachers and Writers Collaborative, 1987.

Paschal, Huston, ed. *The Store of Joys: Writers Celebrate the North Carolina Museum of Art's Fiftieth Anniversary*. Winston-Salem, N.C.: North Carolina Museum of Art, 1997.

Penny, David W. *Art of the American Indian Frontier*. Seattle: University of Washington Press, 1992.

Protherough, Robert. *Encouraging Writing*. London: Methuen, 1983.

Pumphrey, Richard. *Elements of Art*. Upper Saddle River, N.J.: Prentice-Hall, 1996.

Richardson, John Adkins. *Art: The Way It Is*. New York: Harry N. Abrams, 1992.

Rico, Gabriele Lusser. "Daedalus and Icarus Within: The Literature/Art/Writing Connection." *English Journal* (March 1989): 14–23.

Rogers, Franklin R. *Painting & Poetry: Form, Metaphor, and the Language of Literature*. Lewisburg, Pa.: Bucknell University Press, 1985.

Ruskin, Judith A., ed. *Blues Remedy*. (Student Writings about Art) Detroit: Detroit Institute of Arts, 1996.

———. *A Crazy Quilt*. (Student Writings about Art) Detroit: Detroit Institute of Arts, 1997.

————. *Listen to How Great I Will Be*. (Student Writings about Art) Detroit: Detroit Institute of Arts, 1993.

————. *Thunderous Words*. (Student Writings about Art) Detroit: Detroit Institute of Arts, 1994.

St. Clair, Phillip. "A Wilderness with a Map: Teaching the First Course in Creative Writing." *Iowa English Bulletin* 35 (1987): 43–55.

Sebranek, Patrick Verne Meyer, and Dave Kemper. *Writers Inc.: A Student Handbook for Writing and Learning*. Wilmington, Mass.: Write Source, 1996.

Smith, James A., and Dorothy M. Park. *Word Music & Word Magic: Children's Literature Methods*. Boston: Allyn and Bacon, 1977.

Stafford, Barbara Maria. *Symbol and Myth: Hubert de Superville's Essay on Absolute Signs in Art*. London: University of Delaware Press, 1979.

Stewart, Susan. *On Longing: Narratives of the Miniature, the Gigantic, the Souvenir, the Collection*. Baltimore: Johns Hopkins University Press, 1984.

Svendsen, Louise Averill. *Rousseu, Redon, and Fantasy*. New York: Solomon R. Guggenheim Foundation, 1968.

Tham, Hilary. "Poetic Justice: Ekphrasis, Now." *Potomac Review* 8 (fall 1998).

Timbal-Duclaux, Louis. *L'Ecriture Creative*. Paris: Editions Retz, 1986.

Tompkins, Jane P. *Reader-Response Criticism: From Formalism to Post-Structuralism*. Baltimore: Johns Hopkins University Press, 1980.

Troccoli, Joan Carpenter. *First Artist of the West: George Catlin Painting and Watercolors*. Tulsa, Okla.: Gilcrease Museum, 1993.

Truettner, William H. *The Natural Man Observed: A Study of Catlin's Indian Gallery*. Washington, D.C.: Smithsonian Institution Press, 1979.

Updike, John. *Just Looking: Essays on Art*. New York: Alfred A. Knopf, 1989.

Wilhoit, Stephen. "Moffett and Point of View: Creative Writing Assignment Sequence." *Journal of Teaching Writing* 5 (fall 1986): 297–305.

Williams, Raymond. *Keywords: A Vocabulary of Culture and Society*. New York: Oxford University Press, 1983.

Wilmerding, John. *American Art*. New York: Penguin, 1976.

Word as Image: American Art 1960–1990. Milwaukee, Wis.: Milwaukee Art Museum, 1990.

Young, Art, and Toby Fulwiler. *Writing across the Disciplines: Research into Practice*. Upper Montclair, N.J.: Boynton/Cook Publishers, 1986.

Index

About the Author

Throughout her career as museum educator and author, Kathy Walsh-Piper has presented ideas for integrated learning experiences. Throughout her work in several art museums she has championed the development of teacher programs and resources. Ms. Walsh-Piper created interdisciplinary teaching guides for the St. Louis Art Museum and the Art Institute of Chicago and oversaw the development of the Teacher Institute at the National Gallery of Art. In 1984, she was elected as the first Museum Educator of the Year by the National Art Education Association.

She specializes in teaching about works of art through inquiry and creative writing. "For me, the process of writing frees the imagination and puts people in touch with their natural capacity for visual thinking. A skilled teacher has only to ask the right questions, and lead the process." She has presented these teaching methods at museums and conferences across the country.

A native of Chicago, Ms. Walsh-Piper taught for seven years in St. Louis area schools before entering the museum profession. She began her writing career with articles in teaching journals. She is currently director of the University of Kentucky Art Museum.